The 90th Anniversary Publications are available in digital form for free through First Fruits Press. They can be found by visiting First Fruits' Website, under the Heritage Collection: place.asburyseminary.edu/firstfruits

Asbury Theological Seminary 90th Anniversary Publications

Henry Clay Morrison
"Crusader Saint"
by Percival A. Wesche

A Short History of Asbury Theological Seminary
by Howard Fenimore Shipps

The Distinctive Emphases of Asbury Theological Seminary
by Harold B. Kuhn

Theological Foundations
Fiftieth Anniversary Scholarly Essays

All Things Are Ours...
Photographic Record of Asbury's Fiftieth Year

Asbury Theological Seminary 90th Anniversary Publications

Audio Recordings from the 50th Anniversary Celebration
and Special Lecture Series
March 11-15, 1974

50th Anniversary Banquet Speeches
*by Franklin D. Morrison, Frank Bateman Stanger, and
J. C. McPheeters*

*"Salvation Today," "Ingredients of the Gospel,"
"The Mind of Christ," and "Keep the Hope of Heaven"
by Bishop Roy C. Nichols*

*"Whither Wesleyan Theology?" in four parts
by Dr. Albert C. Outler*

*"Whiter Christology?" in four parts
by Dr. C.F.D. Moule*

*"Whither Mission?" in four parts
by Bishop Stephen Neill*

Henry Clay Morrison

"Crusader Saint"

Percival A. Wesche

First Fruits Press
Wilmore, Kentucky
c2013

ISBN: 9781621711063

Henry Clay Morrison "Crusader Saint" by Percival A. Wesche
First Fruits Press, © 2013 | Seminary Press, ©1963

Digital version at http://place.asburyseminary.edu/firstfruitsheritagematerial/24

First Fruits Press is a digital imprint of the Asbury Theological Seminary, B.L. Fisher Library. Asbury Theological Seminary is the legal owner of the material previously published by the Pentecostal Publishing Co. and reserves the right to release new editions of this material as well as new material produced by Asbury Theological Seminary. Its publications are available for noncommercial and educational uses, such as research, teaching and private study. First Fruits Press has licensed the digital version of this work under the Creative Commons Attribution Noncommercial 3.0 United States License. To view a copy of this license, visit http://creativecommons.org/licenses/by-nc/3.0/us/.

For all other uses, contact:

First Fruits Press
B.L. Fisher Library
Asbury Theological Seminary
204 N. Lexington Ave.
Wilmore, KY 40390
http://place.asburyseminary.edu/firstfruits

Wesche, Percival A., 1912-
   Henry Clay Morrison, crusader saint / Percival A. Wesche.
   vi, 241 p. ; 21 cm.
   2nd ed. / revised by Faith E. Parry and Robert Danielson
   Wilmore, Ky. : First Fruits Press, c2013.
   Asbury Theological Seminary 90th Anniversary Publications ; no. 1
   Originally published: Wilmore, Ky. : Seminary Press, c1960.
   ISBN: 9781621711063 (pbk.)
   1. Morrison, H. C. (Henry Clay), 1857-1942. 2. Methodist Church (U.S.) – Kentucky
   – Biography. 3. Clergy – Kentucky – Biography. I. Title. II. Series
BX8495.M68 W4 2013   287.09

Cover design by Kelli Dierdorf

asburyseminary.edu
800.2ASBURY
204 North Lexington Avenue
Wilmore, Kentucky 40390

Henry Clay Morrison

"Crusader Saint"

Percival A. Wesche

Seminary Press
Wilmore, Kentucky
c1963

Preface

No observance of the anniversary of the founding of a graduate school of theology would be complete without significant publications. The Fortieth Anniversary Committee is pleased to present to the friends of Asbury Theological Seminary this significant trilogy of books: *Henry Clay Morrison Crusader Saint, The History of Asbury Theological Seminary,* and *The Distinctive Emphases of Asbury Theological Seminary.*

We congratulate the members of the Fortieth Anniversary Editorial Committee—Dr. Harold B. Kuhn, chairman, Dr. J. Harold Greenlee, and Dr. George A. Turner—for their excellent work, and we commend to you the careful reading of these three significant Fortieth Anniversary volumes.

> Frank Bateman Stanger
> President of the Seminary and
> General Chairman of the Fortieth
> Anniversary Committee

Table of Contents

Preface i

Introduction v

Chapter 1 Boyhood Days 1

Chapter 2 Circuit Rider Days 25

Chapter 3 Years as a Station Pastor 33

Chapter 4 Publishing a Religious Paper 51

Chapter 5 Twenty Years of Evangelism 67

Chapter 6 In Trouble with the Methodist Church ... 87

Chapter 7 First Presidency of Asbury College 101

Chapter 8 Expanding Influence 121

Chapter 9 Second Presidency of Asbury College ... 131

Chapter 10 Under the Cloud of Ill Health 139

Chapter 11 Founding Asbury Theological Seminary ... 151

Chapter 12 Sunset Years 173

Chapter 13 Theological Emphasis 185

Chapter 14 An Influential Life 213

Introduction

For more than half a century the name Henry Clay Morrison was a familiar one in the "holiness movement." From my early youth he was upheld by members of my family as an exemplary preacher. It was as his name was mentioned in prayer at our family altar that I received my personal call to the Christian ministry. Brief acquaintance with Morrison during his intermittent visits to the campus while I was a student at Asbury Theological Seminary increased my interest in knowing more about this man.

The two full-length books purporting to tell his life's story left me feeling as though I had been presented torn fragments of a picture, many parts of which were still missing. The discovery, in 1946, of Morrison's diaries opened the door of research in an effort to answer my questions. This research culminated in a doctoral dissertation, "The Life, Theology, and Influence of Henry Clay Morrison," presented to the Graduate Faculty of the University of Oklahoma. The present publication is based entirely upon the previous research.

I am greatly indebted to the officials of the Pentecostal Publishing Company, Asbury College, and Asbury Theological Seminary for the many courtesies they have shown me. I also wish to express appreciation to my major professor, Dr. John S. Ezell and to Dr. Alfred B. Sears, also of the history department of the University of Oklahoma. My greatest debt, however, is to my wife, Marjorie MacKellar Wesche. Without her moral support and encouragement both in the original research and now during the period of re-writing, the work could not have been brought to completion.

Percival A. Wesche
Nampa, Idaho
July, 1963

Chapter 1
Boyhood Days

If the possession of an honorable ancestry is a real asset then Henry Clay Morrison should have started life in a highly favored position. According to their family tradition the word "Morrison" was derived from "Morris" who was the founder of one of the Highland clans in Scotland. It was developed from the name "Mores," which was the name of the grandson of a Norwegian king who was supposed to have been among the Norse invaders of Scotland.[1]

Morrison's ancestors moved from Scotland to Ireland, and it was from this country that his great-great-grandfather, John O. Morrison, migrated to the American Colonies in time to join the Patriots in the Revolutionary War. He gave his life for this cause in the Battle of Brandywine. The great-grandfather, William Ogden Morrison, migrated to Virginia and settled on a large acreage in Barren County, Kentucky, near what is now the city of Glasgow. Not being content to live in the rough frontier fashion he built one of the first brick houses to be constructed in that section of the country. It was on a portion of this large farm that William B. Morrison was living when he opened his home to two orphaned grand-children, Emma and Henry Morrison.

A glance at the maternal lineage does not change the character of Morrison's ancestry. Great-great-grandfather John Durham was of English stock. Coming to this country he settled first in Virginia, but later migrated to central Kentucky, where he established his home in the Bluegrass Region of Boyle County. He was a devout Methodist and "it was in his home that the first Methodist Society in Kentucky was organized." The Durham family grew and prospered until they became wealthy slave owners. Emily, the mother of Henry Morrison, was the daughter of Thomas Durham. She was born in Danville, Kentucky, and was reared in a devout Methodist home, which was known as "the haven for the circuit riders."[2]

Both of Henry's parents had been previously married. His father, James Scott Morrison married a Miss Blake. She died when their son Charles was three years old. As a young woman, Emily Durham had met and married William H. English, a member of a prominent Indiana family. They made their home in Westport, Kentucky, where their four children were born. Some time after her husband's death, Emily met and later married James Morrison. It was into this household that the subject of this study was born.

Four children were born into the Morrison family, only two of whom lived to grow to maturity; a sister, Emma, who made her appearance on March 14, 1855, and Henry Clay, who was born on March 10, 1857. The baby son was only three weeks old when he was first left by his mother in the care of a kind neighbor lady in order that she might attend the regular quarterly meeting in the old Hickory Grove Methodist Church near Bedford. A neighbor later related how upon Emily Morrison's return she picked up the baby and while weeping, laughing, and praising God said, "Today while I was at church I gave my little Henry Clay to God to preach the Gospel, and I believe that He accepted the gift and when I am dead and gone this baby boy, grown into manhood, will preach Jesus."[3] Although Morrison was not able to remember his mother, he felt he owed her a debt of gratitude because of her devotion to God. "Through the years," he once said, "I have thanked God that my mother gave me to Him in my boyhood to preach Jesus to a lost world."[4]

Two short years of happiness in the Morrison home ended with the death of Henry's mother. Henry and his sister were taken in by grandfather Morrison who was living near Glasgow, Kentucky. James Morrison was engaged in the business of driving mules South for sale and thus was gone from home much of the time. Henry remembered seeing his father only once. He has given the following graphic account of this meeting.

> We climbed over the yard fence and ran down the road, my sister gaining on me for two reasons being older she could run faster, and I ran with some hesitation. I had not the slightest memory of my father, having been separated from him when I was a mere baby, and having not seen him now for two years, and I was not quite sure that it was he. But when he saw us coming he leaped out of the wagon and ran for me. I remember how he looked, the kind of hat he had on; there were tears in his eyes, and laughter in his face; his arms were wide open, and I ran into them.[5]

His father remained with them for a week during which time young Henry was with him almost constantly. The sad day of parting soon came, and James Morrison left for the South with another drove of mules. His first letter spoke of the coming war, of his plan to wind up his business, and to return home as quickly as possible. The prospect of his early return made the children happy, the coming of a war being not an unmixed evil if it would bring their father home again. Instead of the anticipated return, a letter edged in black brought sorrow to the Morrison household. When little Henry inquired the cause of the grief,

> Lizzie took me up in her arms, and after somewhat suppressing her feelings said: "Buddy, your father is dead." A great pain shot through my heart. I leaped from her lap and sought for some one I never found.
>
> For a time it seemed that all possibility of hope and happiness had fled forever. We ate our food in silence, and if the older members of the family looked on us desolate little ones, the tears rolled down their cheeks. Somehow a child's heart will cling to hope, and for a time we looked for a letter contradicting the sad news, and many times at the setting of the sun we gazed long and wistfully up the road for the one that never came.[6]

The death of his father near Vicksburg, Mississippi, left Henry an orphan in his grandfather's home, with only Aunt Lizzie to extend to him anything like a mother's love.

> Being reared in the log house, built on the hillside along the Tompkinsville road a few miles out of Glasgow, carried with it assets as well as liabilities. Although his grandfather was a poor man he had a comfortable home. There was an ample supply of wholesome food. The fall of the year signified butchering time with plenty of hams stored in the log smokehouse. The coming of frost frequently meant that a young heifer would be killed-thus tender beef was added to the

menu. Turnips, cabbage, beets, parsnips, potatoes, and apples were placed in trenches, covered with straw and banked with earth. In this manner vegetables were kept throughout the winter. The Morrisons had little money; however they needed but little to live both comfortably and happily.

William Morrison was a faithful Baptist who held to the firm principles of Calvinism. In the home there was an atmosphere of rigid and unswerving honesty; where deceit and pretense were impossible, where reverence for all things sacred was based upon some of the fundamental tenets of Calvinism. The principles imbibed from the atmosphere of his grandfather's home were no doubt responsible, in part at least, for the stern moral precepts, which governed Morrison's later life.

Some of the most vivid impressions of Morrison's youth came through experiences connected with the Civil War. Although no important battles were fought in the immediate vicinity, the excitement and confusion of those years made a profound imprint upon the emotional, imaginative mind of little Henry. Two times of great fright stood out prominently in the memory of Morrison. The first occurred while watching two companies of would-be Union soldiers drill in a field near his grandfather's farm. Neither group had been issued any equipment by the government so the men were carrying any sort of firearms obtainable. When both sides began firing their guns into the air, little Henry thought so much noise could mean nothing less than a real battle. He raised a terrific cry to go home. His grandfather comforted, scolded, and punished, but to no avail. There was no consoling him until they were both up on the back of old Pickett heading for home.

The second wartime fright was connected with an actual incident of the conflict. A section of the Southern army had captured some raw recruits training for the North. The victorious rebels returned with their prisoners and, in the spirit of jubilation over one of the first victories of the war, fired volleys into whatever targets presented themselves along the road. Of his connection with this event Morrison wrote:

> When I heard the guns, I was frightened and hid in a log loom house that had a little window by one log being sawed out to let in light and air. I was full of fear watching the soldiers pass with the light shining on their muskets. But a group of them came up to the bars of the front of our orchard, which lay about the house, dropped a bar and began to climb over to get some apples. I was sure that was the end for me. I let go and gave way my hiding place. My Aunt Lizzie had a time trying to assure me that the soldier boys were only after apples and that I need not fear.[7]

The nearest Morrison came to seeing a real battle was when General Braxton Bragg was marching northward from Tennessee, in October 1862, prior to the famous battle of Perryville. A large part of his army marched by the Morrison farm. One regiment had been left behind to gather the sick and straggling soldiers and take them along. Just as they got to the farmhouse, news came that "Yankee soldiers were coming into Glasgow as thick as Pigeons." The Southern regiment halted and the officers gathered for counsel in the barn. It was finally decided to build breastworks out of fence rails on the top of Morrison Hill, the location on which the Morrison Camp ground now stands. Preparations were made for battle. The Morrisons were ordered to hide in the nearby woods when the battle started. The family remained fully dressed throughout the night. Aunt Lizzie fixed quilts and blankets to take into the woods and Henry held tightly to his first pair of redtop boots, which he was determined to carry along if flight became necessary. Upon learning that his cavalry was not following in his wake the Colonel retreated during the night toward Tompkinsville. By morning the soldiers were all gone, having left frying pans and coffee pots on smoldering campfires. The horse that the courier had ridden in search for the cavalry was so completely winded that he could not retreat and was left nickering under a persimmon tree. They named him "Bragg" and he became a fairly good farm horse—compensating in part for the fence rails, which the soldiers had burned in their campfires. After the battle of Perryville, Don Carlos Buell's army followed close after the Confederate forces on their retreat toward Chattanooga. For three days and nights the road in front of the Morrison home was so jammed with infantry, cavalry, and baggage trains that it was impossible to get across the road to milk the cows in the near-by pasture. "The cows, however, did not suffer from want of milking. It was very kind of the soldiers to see that their udders were not spoiled from neglect of milking."[8]

While Glasgow never became a real battle area, the people suffered some of those privations in food and clothing, which are common to war. Coffee, for example, became so scarce that people cut raw sweet potatoes into long strips, dried, parched, and ground them and used it in making what was called "coffee." Since no sugar was available "long sweetening" was used. This was sorghum molasses poured into sweet potato coffee. Because clothing became both scarce and expensive most of the boys seven or eight years of age went barefoot during the summer and wore only one garment. It consisted of a long white robe "made of unbleached domestic, with a big collar, long sleeves, and a skirt that reached halfway below our knees; it was split on the sides so as to give our limbs good room for exercise in case a retreat became necessary"[9] Such clothing was found to have advantages for upon going to bed the boys needed only to wash their feet, and all that was necessary to prepare for breakfast in the morning was to wash their faces. "We learned," said Morrison, "that even in the emergency of an awful war our very exigencies might be turned to good account in the way of short cuts and conveniences that we had never known before."[10]

Life on the farm was a co-operative affair. Young "Bud," for so Henry was called in those days, had his assigned duties. Two of these were to keep the wood box and the water-bucket filled. The spring was at the bottom of the hill some distance from the house; therefore he had to stop to rest several times before even a single bucket of water was placed on the shelf in the kitchen. Morrison related that his grandfather never had to tell him when the wood-box or the water-bucket was empty "he would simply look at them, and then look at me. That look was potent, and carried with it imperative orders. He literally guided me with his eye."[11] There was also work to be done in the fields. Even as a little boy Bud could drop grains of corn in the cross of the furrows and learned to kill the cutworms, which might destroy the crop.

The days of Bud's youth were not so crowded with work that no time was left for education or recreation. As a lad he trudged off to school with his sister, she carrying the books and he the "dinner" in a little handmade basket. Bud raced along, much to his sister's disgust, barefooted, with long curly locks and a flushed face which was not always as clean as it might have been by the time they reached the little school house a mile away. According to present standards the curriculum was not entirely adequate since it consisted largely of "McGuffy's Speller." Later, geography and other subjects were added.

The many hours spent in hunting and fishing were a great delight, as well as being helpful in other ways. Game was plentiful, especially after 1865, for there was very little hunting during the war when people did not like to hear the sound of guns. If one of the boys did not get his work done by the time the rest of his neighborhood chums were ready, they would all help with the unfinished chores, and then off they would go for a Saturday afternoon in the woods. During these youthful expeditions, hard times came upon the rabbits, squirrels, partridges, opossums, raccoons, foxes, and skunks.

The farming community in which the Morrisons lived was composed of a neighborly, kindhearted, peace loving, and religious people. Denominational differences seemed to be forgotten during revival meeting times; Baptists and Methodists all joined together in the effort to convert sinners. When anyone became a "mourner" other members of the family would take up his or her household duties, such as chopping the wood, milking the cows or doing the cooking, in order to permit the seekers to hide away upstairs or to slip away into the silent woods to weep over past sins and to call upon God for mercy. "The Bible, the Lord Jesus, sin and salvation, heaven and hell, were wonderfully real among our people. To dance put one out of the church, and to chop wood on Sunday, or to do any kind of work except the most necessary was a disgrace to anyone in the community."[12]

It is little wonder that having been reared in such an atmosphere, Henry Morrison had a keen sense of conviction for sins even when still a young boy. At times some of the boys in the neighborhood would induce him to go to the woods with them for a Sunday afternoon of sport. When the boys had gone and the excitement was over, Henry would hurry to his grandfather's house trembling with fear because of his sins. Many a night his Aunt Lizzie sat up long after other members of the family had retired, holding him on her lap trying to soothe and comfort him. "She would say: 'The child is nervous, and it makes him very restless at night.' The truth was, the Holy Spirit was convicting me of sin. I think I passed through these seasons of fear, all the way from my sixth year up to the time of my conversion..."[13]

When Henry was thirteen, the Rev. James Phillips became pastor of the Boyd's Creek Methodist Church. During the first revival meeting under his ministry a number of Henry's schoolmates, and also his sister Emma, went to the altar of prayer and there found forgiveness of sins and salvation in Christ. Henry was also under deep conviction and wanted to go to the altar, but since he was small for his age he felt that people would think he was too young to know what he was doing. When the sermon was over and the invitation was given, members of the congregation would go throughout the audience inviting others to the mourner's bench. Henry would sit close to the front hoping that someone would speak to him, though no one ever did. When the revival closed he still had a deep conviction for sin; moreover, he felt a sense of disappointment as though people regarded him as a poor little orphan boy who was not even worth inviting to the altar.

Within a few weeks this sensitivity over his sinful separation from God had abated, but the feeling of being considered worthless and of having been neglected lingered on until it became a potent factor in leading him into still more sinful practices. The following spring as Henry was plowing corn on the hillside, where the Morrison Park Campground now stands, it seemed as though Satan walked along with him and made it appear that he was Henry's only real friend. The winsomeness of the appeal can be seen through Morrison's graphic presentation of Satan's soliloquy:

> Well, nobody asked you to the altar. You are a young man, an orphan boy; you have no parents, no money, and nobody cares for you. Time and again you went up and sat near the

front of the church hoping that someone would speak to you, but no one came. It was an outrage that you should be overlooked like this, and if I were you I would get even with them. I'd make them sorry. I would swear and drink whiskey and carry a pistol and fight and make these people regret that they didn't get you saved while you were a boy.[14]

For a time Henry succumbed to such psychic entreaties toward evil and began cursing when outside the hearing of his family. He had never done this before, but now he cursed the stock, the plow, or anything that might arouse his anger. He was so yielding to his tempter that he debated in his own mind whether to be a "fairly decent sinner or something of a desperado."[15] At times, however, his conscience smote him deeply, and in answer to this inner appeal for more righteous living, he made a covenant with God that if the Rev. James Phillips were returned to the circuit for another year he would earnestly seek God. In due time the pastor was returned and Henry anxiously awaited the first revival services.

Protracted meetings were held in the Boyd's Creek Methodist Episcopal Church, South, during Christmas week of 1870. The district school term was so nearly complete that the teacher decided to give only Christmas day as vacation and to teach two or three days following in order to finish. Henry was working hard for a prize which he had a good prospect of winning. During the first part of the week he solved his inner conflict by studying diligently, attending school instead of the services during the day, and going to church at night. School closed Thursday and on the way home that afternoon he told his friend, James Bowles, that he intended to go to the altar that night and "seek religion." True to his word, he was in church that evening, sitting next to the aisle in the third pew from the front. He hoped that by sitting close someone would invite him to go forward for prayer, though he was determined to go alone if no one asked him. Finally the sermon was over and the call given. No one came to him. His struggle was intense. It seemed as though he were riveted to the spot, with all powers of locomotion forever gone. Finally, with a mighty surge he broke away and fairly ran to the altar. Here he began to pray, fully expecting to be converted that night. He felt that he had not been nearly as wicked as had some other boys, and, furthermore; being an orphan boy he should merit some special favor from God. To his genuine surprise, instead of joy and peace, a heavy load seemed to settle down on his heart.

The next two days were a time of heart-searching prayer. He attended meetings both morning and evening and at each knelt at the "mourner's bench," calling upon the Lord for mercy. Sunday morning he rode his horse to the church, arriving there at an early hour. Only about a dozen people were present when he went forward and knelt in front of the old box pulpit, remaining there throughout the entire service. When the preaching was over, sinners were called to the altar and were converted. Henry prayed on, making many promises to the Lord as to what he would do for Him and His cause if only He would bring forgiveness of sins. Finally, after all had gone from the little log church except his sister, Emma, and the Rev. Mr. Phillips, the now discouraged Henry also went home, wondering whether he had sinned away his day of grace.

During the afternoon rain clouds gathered and to Henry the atmosphere seemed dark both without and within. His grandfather said, "My son, you must not go to church tonight. You have been out many nights of late, and it will rain tonight. You will be sick if you get wet."[16] Because Henry felt that he would surely die if he could not get to church that night, he found a place of prayer in the chimney corner. Here he went on three different occasions beseeching the Lord to drive the dark clouds from the sky. Just as the sun was setting the clouds were lifted and a flood of sunlight broke through. Henry ran to his grandfather to get his permission to attend church, and before the weather could change, or his grandfather could alter his mind, Henry mounted his pony and rode off to the revival meeting.

He was late in arriving at the church, the service had begun and he found that the "mourner's bench" was already full of seekers. He found a place of prayer, however, next to the wall on the front seat, in what was usually the "amen" corner. At the close of the service friends tried to encourage him by telling how others were finding peace and salvation. This brought only renewed grief, however, for he felt that if the Lord were so near as to save these others and yet not him there was surely but little hope left. Morrison gave testimony to the subsequent experience:

> Up to this time I had feared that I might be lost. Now I saw clearly that I was lost. I pushed back from the bench and lay down upon the floor, and it seemed that I was "sinking down, sinking down, beneath God's righteous frown." I remember that I felt if I should be lost forever, that God is just. I was wailing aloud, when an old gentleman by the name of Hammer came to me. He was an exemplary member of the Baptist Church, and uncle of my father's by marriage. He stooped down, and in a most tender voice said: "God is not mad at you." The words shot through me. "God loves you," said he, and I ceased to weep "why, God so loved you that he gave his only Son to die for you," said the good man. His words penetrated me,

> and it seemed as if my soul, or a voice within me said, "That is so!" and in an instant I was on my feet praising God. My whole heart was aglow with love. I leaped for joy. Mike Smith, a neighbor boy, was sitting on the step of the pulpit. I caught him about the neck and hugged him with all my might; it seemed that I would die of joy if some vent of expression could not be found. Everybody looked beautiful; all my heart was aglow with love.[17]

This spiritual conversion came to Morrison during the last week of December 1870, when he was thirteen years of age. The knowledge of Christ as a personal Savior was never lost from that night on. He was later baptized by immersion in Boyd's Creek, which flowed back of the church, and was accepted into membership of the Methodist Episcopal Church, South.

Living the Christian life brings struggles as well as blessings. Henry Morrison was neither exempt from the one nor deprived of the other. Soon after his conversion he felt called to establish a family altar in his grandfather's home. Although William Morrison was a staunch Baptist he had never led the family in prayer. At first Henry tried to satisfy his heart by kneeling near his grandfather each evening and offering his own quiet prayer; however, this did not satisfy the call within. The inner struggle became so great that he finally resolved to at least try. The following is his account of the incident:

> When supper was over, I went to a fence corner in the yard and wrestled in prayer for grace and strength to erect the family altar that night. I walked up and down the fence, praying first in this and then in that corner, until it seemed that my soul's salvation depended on my taking up

> the Cross that very night. So I hurried in, and, setting a lamp on the table, got the Bible and turned to the short Psalm I had marked: "You must not read any more tonight, you have read so much of late it has made you nervous," said my grandfather! "I will only read a Psalm" was my answer. "Very well," said he. So I read it, and, closing the book, said: "Let us pray." The family were all frightened, but all dropped on their knees in a hurry. The Lord gave me a wonderful blessing that night. I wept and rejoiced, and came up from my knees with victory over Satan, which has stood me in good stead with the passing of the years.[18]

Some years later, after the death of his grandfather, he became convinced that there should be morning as well as evening prayers. He did not know just how Aunt Lizzie and his sister, Emma, would take this, so one morning he called into their bedroom and said, "I will go to the kitchen and build a fire. While I'm gone you get up and dress and I'll come back and we'll have prayers."[19] Beginning the day by reading from God's written word, and then kneeling down and speaking to Him, proved to be a great spiritual blessing.

Shortly after his conversion Henry felt a call to the ministry. Although he made no attempts at preaching for nearly eight years, he quickly became active in church work. He was frequently called upon to lead in prayer or to speak in testimony meetings, "and it was understood throughout the community that 'Bud Morrison' was going to preach."[20] He and Mike Smith, a boy several years older than he, made it a habit to attend prayer meetings and revivals together. They sat on the front bench, and sometimes wept and rejoiced while the minister preached. As soon as the call to penitents was given, Mike would go down one aisle and Henry another, urging the boys to go to the mourner's bench. "After a while people would say, 'things will move now. Mike Smith and Bud Morrison's come.'"[21]

By the time he was fifteen his grandfather's health had so failed that the major responsibility for the farm work fell upon Henry's young shoulders. With the help of a small Negro boy he cut and hauled the winter's wood, built the fires, cared for the stock, did the plowing, and sowed and harvested the crops. Perhaps it was during these lonely hours in the field that he developed the vivid imagination, which proved to be such an asset in later life.

It was about a year later, when Henry was sixteen that his grandfather died and left him as the head of the family. For another year he worked from dawn till dusk trying to do the necessary work on the farm. The country schools were of about three months duration and he tried to attend, but frequently found it was necessary to miss school in order to tend the farm.

The welcome visit of his half-brother, Captain Thomas English, and his half-sister, Mrs. John Meyer, brought another change into the lives of Henry and Emma Morrison. It was not difficult for Thomas to convince Aunt Lizzie that she should let him take the two young people with him to central Kentucky. It was arranged that Emma should return with him, and she was at once placed in a boarding school. Henry was to remain on the farm near Glasgow until the crops had been gathered in the fall of 1874, after which he was to live near Perryville. "In the late fall," Morrison later wrote, "Aunt Lizzie bought me a suit of store clothes, packed my belongings in a pair of saddle bags, and I mounted a pony which I had raised and started for the Bluegrass."[22]

The next four years were spent in Boyle County near Perryville. During the winter months he lived with his half-sister, Mrs. John Meyer and attended the Ewing Institute. The summer months were spent either in working on the large plantation of his half-brother, Thomas English, or by hiring out to various farmers in the community. Farm labor was cheap. His wages ranged from eight to ten dollars per month, plus room and board.

A debating society was organized at Perryville in connection with the Good Templar Lodge. Henry Morrison was one of the debaters. His speeches were prepared and practiced while trudging between the plow handles. One night each week he walked several miles into Perryville to debate, and won every time. The excitement of public speaking seemed to so exhilarate him that he would return home rested. This feeling of stimulation when speaking before an audience continued throughout his life. So successful was he as a debater that the people of Perryville began to say, "If we do not license Henry Morrison to preach he will go to Congress."[23] This was no little boost to the ego of an orphan boy.

His prowess as a debater soon attracted the attention of the Rev. T. F. Taliaferro who was then pastor of the Methodist Church in Perryville. Taliaferro not only asked him to place his membership in the church, but also made use of his talents. It was to him that Henry confided his call to preach. After this the Methodist minister took an even keener interest in Henry. He invited him into his home, loaned him books, and called on him to pray during the revival services. These experiences enriched his spiritual life and renewed his desire to answer his call to the ministry.

The final decision to respond to God's call to Christian service was not without struggle for it took a wild ride on a runaway horse to make final the choice of his life's work. Even though he had a deep interest in church work, the very poor support given the ministry caused him to feel that it would be a good idea to make and lay by a snug sum of money before devoting his life to preaching. He and his cousin Jimmy concluded that the quickest way to make a fortune would be to go into the cattle business in Texas. Of course not having any money on hand it would be necessary to work as cowboys for a time. Before long, however, their attention was diverted to the sale of a wide variety of scenic pictures. Henry and Cousin Jimmy now agreed to send for some cheap samples and to go into the picture business.

On the day that the sample pictures arrived in Perryville, Henry was riding a big, young horse, which he was breaking to the saddle for a neighbor boy. As he rode out of the village with the pictures in a large haversack strapped over his shoulder, the horses became frightened and broke into a frenzied gallop. The rider's left foot was jerked from the stirrup, and he was thrown entirely out of the saddle and was perched precariously on the saddle horn. As they reached the crest of a hill and started down a steep grade, Henry looked at the hard stone pike and felt sure that he would soon be dashed to certain death.

> Right there, in my heart, I entered the ministry, provided that horse ever stopped running, and I was not killed. I lost interest in Texas cattle, and entirely gave up the picture business. I had no desire to be rich. I wanted to be a preacher of the gospel. I lost sight of the financial future; to be a poor, earnest preacher was good enough for me. My decision was full and final. In less than a minute I was firmly seated in the saddle, my horse was under control, and in the

mad dash of those few hundred yards I had been changed from an enterprising cattleman or an extensive dealer in fine art into a humble, contented circuit rider. But for the runaway horse I might have drifted from one adventure to another, and finally fallen away from Christ, never have entered the ministry and, in the end, lost my soul. Thank God for the wild ride that landed me in the ministry.[24]

The Rev. T. G. Taliaferro had encouraged Morrison to enter the ministry ever since his coming to the pastorate of the Perryville Methodist Church. He had licensed Henry as an exhorter and one Sunday during the summer of 1878 he asked the congregation to remain for a short business meeting. At his request the congregation agreed to recommend Henry Morrison to the Quarterly Conference to be licensed as a local preacher. When the vote was taken every person but one, his half brother, Thomas English, voted for the recommendation. As Henry and his brother, Tom, rode home in the buggy, the former received a real tongue-lashing:

> You and Taliaferro have taken snap judgment on me. I didn't know you were going to get a license to preach. You can't preach. If there is anybody that I am not interested in it is a one horse Methodist preacher dragging a woman and children around the country at the point of starvation. We have one scrub preacher among our kinsfolk and that's enough. I stand in with the congressmen of this district and I could have gotten you into West Point and made an army officer out of you, or I could have put you with Judge Durham in Danville to make a lawyer out of you. You could have been somebody of

whom we would feel proud. I was crying bitterly and I said, "But, Tom, you see the Lord has called me to preach." To which he answered, "He must be hard up for material."[25]

During the remainder of the journey home Henry prayed silently for the Lord to help him in his determination to preach regardless of what his brother, Tom, might say. The next Quarterly Conference of the Methodist Episcopal Church, South, in Perryville, Kentucky, having the Rev. D. W. Welburn as Presiding Elder, granted to Henry Morrison a local preacher's license.

Since the close of the conference was at hand it was agreed that the rights granted by the newly acquired license should not be used until Taliaferro reached his new circuit. Soon afterward, however, he was taken sick; therefore he called Henry to preach for him the following Sunday in two of his country appointments: Johnson's Chapel on Rolling Fork River, and Sycamore. After preparing his first sermon Morrison left on Saturday afternoon for his first preaching engagement. Sunday morning Henry arose early and after eating only a little breakfast retired to a thicket on the hillside where he wept and prayed earnestly for a long while. By church time the little Chapel was well filled. The young preacher took his text, "Come unto me, all ye that labor and are heavy laden, and I will give you rest." He soon ran out of anything to say but fell back on his personal testimony, telling of his conviction, conversion, and some of his experiences in the Christian life. It was said that "Everybody in the church wept. Even our schoolteacher who isn't a Christian, and never was known to weep before wept while you preached and told your experiences."[26]

In the afternoon service at Sycamore he spoke from the words, "Repent, for the kingdom of heaven is at hand." He did not succeed as well as he had in the morning and once again fell back on the expedient of relating his personal experiences. The people were understanding of his inexperience and seemed pleased with the service. Recalling this incident later he said, "I was received at the parsonage with great joy, spent the night there, breathed freely and felt that I had been initiated into the ministry."[27]

The Rev. T. F. Taliaferro was so pleased by the reports he received relative to Morrison's preaching that he insisted he should also preach in Perryville, much to the embarrassment of everyone concerned. The church was packed to hear him. To his gratification his sweetheart was also there. At the appointed time he went into the pulpit with an attitude of assurance. He read the same text he had used at Sycamore Chapel, and since he had gotten along fairly well there he felt confident. When, however, he looked up at the large and expectant audience, with two of the leading infidels of the town sitting directly in front of him, every thought he had relating to the text vanished. After a pause which must have seemed like an eternity, he cried out:

> I believe God has called me to preach. I believe that the God of Abraham, Isaac and Jacob has called me to preach, but I cannot preach tonight. I have forgotten everything I wished to say, but I intend to preach. "Woe is me, if I preach not the gospel." I cannot preach now but I will preach later on.

Occasionally he would cry at the top of his voice "Repent, for the kingdom of heaven is at hand."[28] Finally he walked down from the pulpit to the floor of the auditorium exhorting the people as he went. At last, after ten or twelve minutes he called on his old friend, Professor Borden, of the Ewing Institute, to pray. This professor was so mortified over

Morrison's failure that he did not feel in the spirit of prayer, so asked the pastor to pronounce the benediction—which he did. Borden then took Morrison's hand and said, "Henry, my boy, the greatest orator who ever lived failed the first time. Try them again."[29] The humiliated young preacher assured him that he would not give up.

The Rev. T. F. Taliaferro realized that this was a crucial period in the life of his young friend, so insisted that he must preach again in the same place two weeks from that Sunday evening. For this service Henry used the text of his first sermon at Johnson's Chapel, but this time he wrote everything "from text to Amen." At the appointed hour another large audience had gathered. Morrison put his manuscript on the pulpit and read it word for word. Although his sermon was not the failure of two weeks before, it lacked the warmth of spirit and effectiveness of his first sermon. After returning to the parsonage he said:

> Brother Taliaferro, we've made a mistake. When I went over to Johnson's Chapel where there was need that I preach I had liberty and was blessed. Here you are putting me up where there's no need for it and I am trying to show the people that I can reach, and I am a pitiful failure. Don't ask me to preach any more unless there is a call for it, a reason why I should go into the pulpit to deliver a message from the Lord.[30]

This was his last attempt, as a young man, to preach in Perryville. Under the encouraging tutelage of T. F. Taliaferro he was soon seen, however, as a junior preacher riding the Floydsburg Circuit.

Notes

[1] H. C. Morrison, *Some Chapters of My Life Story* (Louisville, 1941). Hereafter referred to as *Some Chapters of My Life Story*.

[2] *The Pentecostal Herald.*

[3] *Ibid.*

[4] *Some Chapters of My Life Story.*

[5] C. F. Wimberly, *A Biographical Sketch of Henry Clay Morrison, D.D.* (Chicago, 1922). Digital copy freely available from First Fruits Press: <http://place.asburyseminary.edu/firstfruitsheritagematerial/7/> Hereafter referred to as *A Biographical Sketch of Henry Clay Morrison.*

[6] *Ibid.*

[7] *The Pentecostal Herald.*

[8] *Ibid.*

[9] *Ibid.*

[10] *Ibid.*

[11] *Ibid.*

[12] *The Ibid.*

[13] *Ibid.*

[14] *Some Chapters of My Life Story.*

[15] *Ibid.*

[16] *The Pentecostal Herald.*

[17] *Ibid.*

[18] *Ibid.*

[19] *Some Chapters of My Life Story.*

[20] *The Pentecostal Herald.*

[21] *Some Chapters of My Life Story.*

[22] *The Pentecostal Herald.*

[23] *A Biographical Sketch of Henry Clay Morrison.*

[24] H. C. Morrison, *Remarkable Conversions, Interesting Incidents, and Striking Illustrations* (Louisville, 1925). Hereafter referred to as *Remarkable Conversions*. Digital copy freely available from First Fruits Press:
<http://place.asburyseminary.edu/firstfruitsheritagematerial/26/>

[25] *Some Chapters of My Life Story.*

[26] *Ibid.*

[27] *The Pentecostal Herald.*

[28] *Ibid.*

[29] *Some Chapters of My Life Story.*

[30] *Ibid.*

Chapter 2
Circuit Rider Days

There have been few if any more picturesque and romantic figures in American history than that of the Methodist circuit rider. Possessed of an indomitable courage and a spirit of abandonment to the cause of the Kingdom of God he went to carry the message to the scattered inhabitants of the frontier. Henry Morrison lived during an interesting transitional period. Although converted by a circuit preacher, and spending three and a half years in that role himself, he lived to see that familiar character become almost the legendary figure of the ignored church history book.

In the fall of 1878, after the Rev. T. F. Taliaferro had been transferred from Perryville to the Floydsburg Circuit, Morrison left farming to devote the remainder of his life to Christian service. Since his first circuit consisted of four churches: Floydsburg, Shiloh, Wesley's Chapel, and Glenmary, a schedule was arranged which enabled Morrison to preach both morning and evening of each Sunday. Not having a horse of his own he walked the circuit until conference met the next fall. The handsome, black-haired young preacher of medium height was frequently seen striding through the streets of the little towns where he served.

It was while traveling on this circuit that he won his first convert to Christ and also received his first pay for preaching. The Rev. T. J. McIntyre was assisting Brother Taliaferro in a revival meeting in the old stone church about eighteen miles out of Louisville. Because of illness in their homes both were called away, and Morrison was asked to preach the three or four nights remaining before the close of the meeting on Sunday. It was in one of these services that a young lady came and knelt at the altar of prayer, where she found Christ as her Savior. Henry had led seekers to the altar may times before and had joined in prayer with others, but this was the first convert as the result of his own preaching. At the close of the conference year the various churches of the Quarterly Conference made up and handed to him thirty-four dollars for his services during the six months.

In September 1879, Morrison attended his first Annual Conference in Richmond, Kentucky. Since he was not a member of the Conference he fully intended to spend the coming year as he had the last few months, but the new Presiding Elder of the Shelbyville District, the Rev. J. W. Fitch, appointed Morrison to the Jacksonville Circuit as assistant pastor to the Rev. Charles W. Cooper. This was a large circuit consisting of six appointments in three different counties. These congregations had been quite neglected for some years, often not having had any preaching services for long periods of time, with the result that the Methodist work was quite disorganized. Some complained of the appointment of Copper because of his youth and inexperience, he having made only one attempt at preaching previous to this appointment. This accounted in part, at least, for the sending of Morrison as assistant. The Presiding Elder said, "It may be that you two boys can be equal to one man."[1] When Morrison received this appointment he had no horse, purse, watch, or even an extra coat. On the way to Jacksonville he stopped at the home of Dr. Wiley T. Poynter, who was president of Science Hill School for Girls, located in Shelbyville, Kentucky. As the Doctor looked at him, with no money, very little education, and only a borrowed pony he said: "Well, Morrison, there is one consolation in your case; if you make nay change, it is sure to be for the better, for you are certainly starting from the bottom."[2]

Although Cooper and Morrison had never seen each other before, they soon became fast friends. The months on this charge were busy and successful ones. Morrison congregations were so large that women and children were forced to sit on the platform and the steps, and the space around the altar was also filled.

It was wile making the necessarily long rides on this circuit that Morrison acquired the habit of drinking coffee. It seems that he had been prejudiced against it through some childhood experiences in which the drinking of a cup of coffee into which a large dose of castor oil had been poured was used as a cure for "cramp colic" – usually caused by eating too many green apples! After yielding to the entreaties of some of the good ladies on the Jacksonville Circuit he found that coffee was not so bad when not adulterated with castor oil. He continued his coffee drinking for five or six years until a kindly doctor suggested that his health would be improved if he would entirely refrain from its use. "I thought the matter over," related Morrison, "and felt that perhaps the doctor was correct, and that as I belonged to the Lord, I could not afford to do anything that would damage my body and hinder a larger and better usefulness; so I quit!"[3] During the last fifty-five years of his life he drank only two cups of coffee, thinking they were postum. He did not condemn others for using it, but felt that the improvement in his health justified him in leaving it alone.

The financial arrangements on the Jacksonville Circuit would not be considered adequate today. No definite salary was promised and no systematic effort was made to raise money for the young preachers. A total of $120 was given during the year, which they divided equally. During the year Morrison's clothing became worn and patched, and it was with difficulty he obtained a decent suit to wear to the Annual Conference, in September 1880. Misfortune was added to poverty; however, when one night toward the close of the year someone stole the little pony he had borrowed from Aunt Kittie Jones. After paying fifty dollars for the stolen horse he did not have much left from his sixty-dollar salary!

Since he was still not a member of the Conference, his appointment as supply to the Westport Circuit was made by the Presiding Elder. This was his first year to have the personal responsibility for the work of a circuit. When he arrived at Buckner's Station, a village near the Glenmary Church, he had neither money nor equipment. He was given a nice room in the office of the village doctor, rent free, and Dave Payne, who was ticket agent on the Louisville and Nashville Railroad, loaned him a small cot and a quilt. By using his overcoat as a cover, Morrison was able to sleep very comfortably except on cold nights. He bought meal tickets at Johnson's boarding house. Because his salary averaged only $11.08 per month, he went to bed without supper at times when the dots remaining on the meal ticket were few in number. By the close of the year he had received $140, bringing his total income for his first two and one-half years in the ministry to about $230. He later facetiously said that his financial inability to buy a watch during the first years of his ministry might have been responsible for the development of his habit of preaching long sermons.

The spiritual aspects of the work were perhaps more encouraging than were the temporal. Revivals were held in each of the three churches, Glenmary, Westport, and Mt. Hebron. It was while Taliaferro was assisting in the Mt. Hebron meeting that Ulysses Grant Foote, a boy who was later to become one of the well-known Southern Methodist pastors, was converted. Morrison's first request to hold a revival meeting outside his own charge came during the summer months while serving this circuit. He responded to the request of W. S. Peoples, a student pastor, to hold revivals in the Cedar Chapel and Tyrone churches, with the result that a number of people were converted and joined the church.

It was during the Annual Conference, which met in Danville in September 1881, that Morrison was admitted to the Conference on trial. Because of illness he was a few days late and unable to appear with the regular class for examination; consequently, he was examined privately by Dr. S. W. Spear, who had been a member of the General Conference at which the Methodist Episcopal Church, South, was organized, and was revered by his associates for both his scholarship and his Christian spirit. Some years later Morrison asked how he had contrived to look favorably upon his examination and pass him. Dr. Spear replied, "Oh, I thought you were a right bright boy and that you would study! I saw you had religion and thought you might develop into a useful preacher."[4]

Since Morrison was now a member of the Kentucky Conference his appointment came from the Bishop, and when the list was read he was assigned to the Concord Circuit. This, his last circuit, consisted of four churches – Concord, Tollsboro, Bethel and Harrison – located along the Ohio River in the extreme northeast part of Kentucky about fifteen or twenty miles above Maysville. Morrison's headquarters for the year were in the home of Mr. and Mrs. Thomas Putman. Their consistent Christian lives so impressed Morrison that one of the buildings at Asbury College, "Putman Hall," was later named in honor of this godly man and his devout wife.

Two interesting experiences which befell him that year are worthy of mention. Shortly after arriving on the circuit he had a severe attack of measles. The amusing part of this incident was that when the Rev. Alec Redd had traveled this circuit a few years before, he had had measles; and just the year previous the Rev. J. W. Hughes had suffered from the same disease. Some of the people said that "Methodist preachers were a 'measly set.'"[5]

The second of the two events was Morrison's acceptance of a dare to swim the Ohio River, which was about a mile wide at that point. The strong current carried him nearly half a mile downstream, but he finally reached the other side, tired, but victorious. "This feat," wrote Morrison later, "did not hurt the size of my congregations the next Sunday. People like to be preached to by a human being. Let him be clean, earnest, fearlessly intent on winning souls, and he can be ever so human, and they will hear him gladly."[6]

From a financial point of view the year on the Concord Circuit exceeded that of his entire previous ministry. With the $340, which he had received, Morrison was able to buy a good horse, a watch, and was very well outfitted in other respects. The presiding elder felt, however, that Morrison was worthy of a better place and so stated while holding the last Quarterly Conference: "Morrison, the time has come to give you a work that will pay you more...if I can find a better appointment for you on my district I will give it to you. If some other Presiding Elder offers a better work than I can give you, I will let you go."[7] These words were more than an idle promise, for Morrison's report to the Kentucky Annual Conference in the fall of 1882 proved to be the last as a Circuit Rider.

Notes

---

[1] *Some Chapters of My Life Story.*

[2] *A Biographical Sketch of Henry Clay Morrison.*

[3] *The Pentecostal Herald.*

[4] *Ibid.*

[5] *Ibid.*

[6] *A Biographical Sketch of Henry Clay Morrison.*

[7] *The Pentecostal Herald.*

Chapter 3
Years as a Station Pastor

The eight years from the fall of 1882 until 1890 constituted a period of rapid advancement in the life of Henry Clay Morrison as a station pastor.[1] During this time he spent one year in Vanderbilt University and served as pastor of five different Methodist churches, each being successively larger and more influential than the previous one.

When the appointments were read on September 12, 1882, by Bishop H. N. McTyeire, Morrison learned that he was assigned to Stanford.[2] This was a county-seat town of about three thousand inhabitants, which had a Methodist church of such size as to require the services of a married man. When Morrison thanked the Bishop for his appointment, McTyeire placed his arm gently around the younger man's shoulder and said: "My young brother, I believe you will do right and the presiding elder believes you will. But there is a female college at Stanford, near your church. There are many young ladies in that school and you must be very judicious."[3]

It was with a feeling of insecurity that Morrison entered his new work. Never before had he so greatly felt the inadequacy of his training. Not only was he following the Rev. J. S. Simms, a graduate of DePauw University, and a man noted for his pulpit ability, but the churchyard joined the campus of

Mrs. Trueheart's famous Female College. The fact that she and many of the other professors were Methodists and thus attended services there, gave to the church a peculiar prominence in the community. Morrison later remarked that, "Most preachers will agree with me that it is a bit embarrassing to preach to college professors."[4]

He especially feared Mrs. Trueheart because she possessed unusual traits of both culture and piety. Somewhat later he said to her: "When I came here, I feared to preach before you, but you are such a good listener that you are really helpful rather than a hindrance to my pulpit ministrations." She smiled and replied, "Well, Mr. Morrison, I learned long ago when I attend preaching to listen very carefully to everything the preacher says. If he is a good preacher, I cannot afford to miss anything he says. If he is a poor preacher, I must give close attention in order to get what little good he does say."[5] Poor Morrison was left with no enlightenment as to which class he belonged! But instead of discouraging him and crippling his future usefulness, this church served as a challenge to his development during the two years of an interesting ministry in the town.

It was during the pastorate at Stanford that Morrison encountered one of the first persons, with whom he had close association, who claimed to have the experience of entire sanctification. Mary McAfee, together with her mother and maiden sister, kept the tollgate on the Crab Orchard Turnpike. Mary was commended for her saintly life by persons of all walks of life, from the pastors of other churches in the town to the Negro boy who attended the service, which Morrison was conducting in the county jail. It is little wonder that she also made a profound impression upon this young Methodist preacher who had not as yet come into the experience of heart holiness—a doctrine, which he was later to espouse with such effectiveness.

In addition to the two good revivals at Stanford during the two years of his stay there, Morrison assisted neighboring pastors in "protracted meetings." The calls to assist in revival meetings, which were to come in such numbers throughout the following years, were already attracting Morrison from his pastoral duties.

Largely through the advice of friends, among whom the Rev. H. B. Cockrill was most influential, Morrison "located" at the close of this second year with the Stanford church, and entered Vanderbilt University in the fall of 1884. This school was situated in Nashville, Tennessee, one of the cultural centers of the South, and the educational and social center of Southern Methodism. Although Morrison had as professors some of the finest scholars in his denomination, his misconception of the real purpose of education led him to a feeling of disappointment. He thought the instructors would help him to make sermons and tell him just how to preach. He expected the professors to put the sharpened sword into his hand and to teach him how to use it to the best advantage, bringing such conviction to the hearts of sinners that they would come running to the altar of prayer. Instead they set him to studying volumes of history and theology that he might gain knowledge to be used in his own thought and sermon preparation. Morrison's inadequate primary and secondary school training now proved a very definite handicap when thrown into classroom competition with men who were college graduates. It was only by constant and diligent study from early morning until late at night that he was able to pass his examinations in all but one subject.

Morrison did not completely refrain from preaching during this year as a college student. Dr. Gross Alexander, the University Chaplain and pastor of the West End Methodist Church where many of the University people worshipped, occasionally called on him to preach in his church. These challenging experiences served to convince Morrison more than ever before that his place was in the active work of the ministry rather than in the academic confines of Vanderbilt University.

The summer of 1885 was spent in revival campaigns. As soon as his class work was completed and his examinations were over, Morrison left Vanderbilt and returned to Stanford, where he assisted the Rev. F. S. Pollitt in a series of special meetings. Soon after the close of the revival there, Morrison received a call to go to Wilmore, Kentucky. The Methodists of the community had just built a new church and had called Dr. R. H. Rivers of Louisville to preach the dedicatory sermon. On the Sunday of the dedication a revival broke out; at least twenty-five persons sought and found Christ as Savior and united with the church. Dr. Rivers sent for Morrison and continued the meetings himself until the younger preacher could arrive. When he got off the train in Wilmore, Morrison found that the village consisted of the new church and three residences. He remained a number of days, preaching twice each day, with the result that 104 persons were converted and joined the church. It was the success of this revival, which attracted the attention of J. W. Hughes to Wilmore when he was seeking a place to erect a holiness college. Upon the invitation of the Rev. W. S. Grinstead, pastor of the church at the time, Hughes bought a small tract of land and opened the school, which was soon to be named Asbury College.

Morrison was engaged in evangelistic work until September, at which time he was readmitted to the conference and was appointed to the Eleventh Street Church in Covington.

This was considered to be a promotion from his former church in Stanford. Aside from carrying forward the work of the charge in such a manner as to warrant promotion at the end of the year, he found time to hold five revival meetings in other churches.

It was while preaching in the regular Sunday morning service at his church in Covington that Morrison was heard by George Spencer, an official of the Hill Street church. Following the service he said: "Henry Clay, I have come after you. Monday morning you are going home with me to begin a revival meeting Monday evening in our church."[6] After some hesitation and embarrassment, for Hill Street was one of the most prominent churches in the conference, Morrison announced in his evening service that he had made arrangements to be away for two weeks. In Lexington he was advertised as a "boy preacher" although he was actually twenty-eight years of age. The meeting continued for three weeks instead of the two originally announced, and might have continued longer had not Morrison's presiding Elder, the Rev. Charles Taylor, written him saying: "Your people are like sheep without a shepherd. You must come home."[7] One other important result of the meeting must not be omitted. At this time Henry met Miss Laura Bain, who was later to become his wife.

It was during the year in Covington that Morrison became convicted for his use of tobacco and discontinued it. Although he had tried chewing tobacco only once in his life, he had become quite addicted to cigars. At that time most of the preachers with whom he was acquainted smoked without compunction of conscience, and he had never given the matter much thought. Now, however, he realized that some of the money he was spending for cigars came from the sacrificial giving of the working girls in his church; thus the habit assumed a new significance. "One night after retiring," he related, "the

Lord had an interview with me on the subject. My conscience was thoroughly aroused and my suffering intense. Then and there I quit tobacco absolutely and forever, and some weeks after, the Lord destroyed all appetite for it."[8] From that time he actively opposed the use of tobacco, especially by members of the clergy.

The Kentucky Annual Conference was held in Winchester in September of 1886. This was the occasion of his ordination as Deacon. As the appointments were read for the year 1886-1887, he learned that he had been transferred to the church in Highlands, Kentucky. This community, later known as Fort Thomas, was located a short distance up the Ohio River from Covington in some beautiful hills overlooking the city of Cincinnati. The church membership was composed of a number of very cultured families. Of particular benefit to Morrison was the privilege of associating with Dr. T. N. Ralston, author of the well-known *Ralston's Elements of Divinity*, who lived near the church.

In spite of the increased responsibilities of a larger congregation, time was also found for conducting several protracted meetings. The outstanding revival of the year was the one held in Winchester during the latter part of February and continuing into March 1887, during the time Dr. J. H. Young was pastor of the Methodist church there. Nearly 150 souls professed salvation; ninety-seven having united with the Methodist church while more than fifty joined other churches in the city. The crowds grew so large that they could not be accommodated in the church, thus the services were moved to the Winchester Opera House where as many as 600 attended a single meeting. Morrison's appeal to the young men of the community was so great that under his leadership a Young Men's Christian Association was formed and a collection of one thousand dollars was taken for the purpose of renting a hall in which to carry on its activities. As a special token of their appreciation the young men who had been converted during the meeting presented the evangelist with a gold watch, which he carried throughout the remainder of his life.

A further result of this revival was the stimulation of interest in the locating of Kentucky Wesleyan College in Winchester. Morrison returned to the city some time later to spend a week holding mass meetings in the Opera House at night and canvassing the business men during the day in an effort to raise money for the college. As a result of the $38,000 subscribed in this campaign the Kentucky Annual Conference accepted a recommendation, which resulted in the moving of Wesleyan College from Millersburg to Winchester in the year 1890.

Another noteworthy revival was that held in Paris, Kentucky, March 21 to April 10, 1887. Attendance outgrew the Methodist Church and services were moved first to the courthouse and later to the large Presbyterian Church. So great was the interest that special trains were run from Lexington to Paris. Morrison's appeal to the young men was similar to that in the earlier meeting in Winchester, with the result that a Young Men's Christian Association was organized in Paris.

Without doubt the outstanding event of the year in Highlands, so far as Morrison was personally concerned, was the religious awakening, which he himself received in experiencing the work of "entire sanctification." During the period of the early 1880's, Dr. W. B. Godbey was the only man in the Kentucky Conference who professed to have had this experience. Later the Rev. John S. Keen, a member of the Louisville Conference came into this state of grace. Thereafter others sought and received this blessing. These professions caused a great deal of discussion among the preachers of the conference concerning sanctification. Morrison, as did many others, held the growth theory. He had been taught by those opposed to the experience of entire sanctification that those who professed it claimed to have obtained a religious experience whereby it was impossible for them to be tempted, to commit sin, or to grow in grace, for they had already attained all the spiritual development that was possible in this life. Even though rejecting the doctrine of holiness, Morrison felt a need for a deeper, more abiding experience with God than he had thus far possessed; therefore he said little against the doctrine or those who claimed to have the experience. Meanwhile, two associates greatly influenced his thinking along this line. The Rev. W. S. Grinstead "claimed to have been wholly sanctified as a second, distinct work of grace."[9] He was a very zealous Christian and his success in the ministry was so remarkable that he commanded the respect of his friends. Morrison secretly wished that he could possess the type of holy zeal and constant joy represented in the life of his co-worker. Horace Cockrill was the other friend who influenced the popular young pastor to study John Wesley's *Plain Account of Christian Perfection* in order to gain a better understanding of the doctrine. After Cockrill received the experience, they spent long hours talking of the change in his spiritual life since receiving "the blessing." When not together they wrote frequently-Cockrill always urging Morrison to "enter in" to this richer spiritual life.

God's gift of a pure heart was finally given to Morrison during the time Dr. J. H. Young was assisting in revival meetings in the Highlands Church. One day they were taking dinner in the home of James Southgate when Morrison received a letter from his friend, Cockrill. Excusing himself he went into the hall to read it, and as he read a new spiritual light began to dawn. Concerning such a vital experience a man should be permitted to give his own testimony.

> ...the truth broke in upon me like an inspiration; I saw the doctrine and experience of full salvation as clearly as the sun in a cloudless noonday sky. My whole heart said, "It is the truth," and I laughed and wept for joy. It seemed as if the following conversation went on within my breast: "I am the Lord's child. Yes but not his holy child. He wants me to be holy, but I cannot make myself holy. That is so, but he can make me holy." "Yes, he can," was the response of my whole heart. I saw clearly the reasonableness of it all, and the will and power of God in the matter. I felt assured that I should return to my boarding house after dinner, go to my room, and receive the blessing as a free gift to God.[10]

Dinner was announced, and after visiting for a time following the eating of the meal, Morrison asked to be excused and started down the street toward his room. At this time he was rooming with Mr. and Mrs. Taliaferro, the parents of the minister who had granted his first local preacher's license. On his way he stopped in four different homes where he had prayer with the families. His heart was aglow with the new assurance for he felt confident that God would soon bestow upon him an evidence of His presence in his life. During one of these pastoral calls Dr. Young passed down the Avenue and went to Morrison's room. When the young pastor arrived at his room his friend suggested that he thought it a good idea to close the meeting for there were few prospects of having a genuine revival. This was so contrary to Morrison's appraisal of the possibility of a spiritual awakening that he remonstrated with the doctor. Morrison has graphically described the subsequent scene.

> "Why, Doctor," said I, "the power of God is all over this hill." Throwing up my hands, I said, "the power of God is in this room; I feel it now." Instantly, the Spirit fell on me and I fell backward on a divan, as helpless as a dead man. I was conscious of the mighty hand of God dealing with me. Dr. Young leaped up, caught me in his arms, and called me again and again, but I was powerless to answer.
>
> Just as I came to myself and recovered the use of my limbs, a round ball of liquid fire seemed to strike me in the face, dissolve, and enter into me. I leaped up and shouted aloud, "Glory to God!" Dr. Young, who still had me in his arms, threw me back on the divan and said, "Morrison, what do you mean? You frightened me. I thought you were dying. Why did you act that way?" "I did not do anything, Doctor," said I, "the Lord did it." I arose and walked the floor, feeling as light as a feather.[11]

Morrison had read but little and had heard but few sermons on the subject of sanctification, and as a consequence knew little about living and testifying to this new state of grace. Under the influence of ministerial associates who did not possess the experience, he was led to believe that to testify to others concerning such a gift from God would seem boastful and would only give offense. As a result he failed to witness to others of his new blessing, and "gradually," he said, "the warm glow left my heart, and I was sadly conscious that my wonderful blessing was gone."[12] It was not until months later, after weeks of intense struggle, that he became firmly established in this spiritual condition.

Morrison's fame as an evangelist was spreading. Before the close of the conference year of 1886-87 so many calls to conduct revivals came to him that his mind was fully made up to "locate" at the next Annual Conference and give his full time to evangelism. He purchased a new trunk and took it, already packed, to the meeting of the Conference in Covington. There about forty of the leading preachers of the conference begged him not to "locate," but to continue in the pastoral ministry at least a few years longer. As a result of this persuasion Morrison remained in the itinerant ministry for another three years, an experience he never regretted.

This Conference had other features, which made it memorable to Henry Morrison. This was the Conference at which he was elected to Elder's Orders and was ordained by Bishop John C. Granberry. For the first time he could now enter upon his ministry as a full-fledged Methodist Elder. Another unusual occurrence was the manner of his appointment to Danville. Presiding Elder Joseph Rand was anxious to have Morrison sent to Frankfort, but there seemed to be more powerful influences at work. Colonel John Proctor came with a request from the official board of the Danville Church that Morrison be appointed there. After remonstrating that the Danville church was too large for such a young man, Morrison promised the Colonel that he would go wherever the Bishop might send him. John Proctor then visited Bishop Granberry where necessary arrangements were made and at the conclusion of the Conference H. C. Morrison was designated as the pastor of the Walnut Street Methodist Church, South, in Danville.

Danville was one of the most cultured and delightful little cities in the state of Kentucky at that time. Centre College and a very fine female college were located there. The church was accustomed to a dignified pastor and though Morrison had the reputation of being a very zealous and eloquent preacher, their adjustment to his evangelistic style was not always easy. During the year two events stand out as being worthy of record in this biography.

The first was the agonizing experience through which Morrison passed before regaining and becoming established in the blessing of entire sanctification, which he had first experienced the previous year. According to his account the Spirit of the Lord frequently spoke to him about his "lost blessing." At times his concern over this situation was so great that he could not sleep at night, therefore he spent the time in prayer. Some help was received through consultation with Dr. Lapsley McKee, a celebrated old Presbyterian minister residing in Danville, who said: "My young brother, the Lord has not forsaken you, but is leading you into what Mr. Wesley called Christian Perfection. The Baptists call it the rest of faith, the Presbyterians the higher life, or fullness of the Spirit." He then went on to testify as to how he had himself received this baptism with the Holy Spirit at the time he was a young pastor in Louisville. Morrison continued his quest for spiritual peace until at last he was satisfied.

> The last day of this soul conflict, I fainted three times. I was boarding with my sister, Mrs. Meyer, I had been down town and finding my strength gone, I stopped at the bank and asked Bro. Will Proctor to walk home with me. We went around to the house, and I stepped in and dropped into an armchair. I was wearing a tall silk hat. I fell backward, and my plug hat fell off, bouncing about the floor. I lost consciousness as it went over the top of the chair. They soon had a doctor with me, and got me up to my bed. Twice more that day I fainted away, and

felt that I would certainly die. It seemed that all of his waves and billows went over me. The next morning while on my knees at a little table reading the letter to the Laodicean Church, while reading these words, *"As many as I love I chasten,"* the light broke in upon me. It seemed as if Jesus spoke the words from his own lips, and my heart was filled with peace and joy. Again, for want of instruction, I failed to testify, and lost my full assurance, and had a conflict more or less severe for many months before I became fully established.[13]

The second memorable event of the year 1888, was Morrison's marriage to Laura Dodd Bain on June 20th. Some of the incidents of this courtship seem so out of harmony with the fearlessness of character, which Morrison demonstrated in other realms of activity that they are of tantalizing interest. According to reports, Henry was seldom without a sweetheart during his youthful days; thus the timidity, which he demonstrated in his early association with Miss Bain, was perhaps not his habitual manner of conduct! It was in 1884, while Morrison was a student at Vanderbilt University that he first heard of Laura Bain. One of his professors, Dr. Thomas Dodd, told of an amusing incident, which had taken place at a baptismal service during the time that he was pastor of the Methodist Church in Paris, Kentucky. Upon inquiry Morrison learned that the baby girl involved in the story was Laura Dodd Bain, daughter of Colonel George W. Bain, a very renowned Chautauqua lecturer who lived in Lexington. After ascertaining when this incident had occurred Morrison said to himself: "When I get back to Kentucky I am going to see that girl. She's old enough now to be in society and to marry, and if she's the worthy daughter of that great man she would be a worthy wife of any Methodist preacher."[14]

During the following year, 1885, while holding a revival in the Hill Street Church in Lexington, the evangelist was invited to take dinner at the home of Colonel and Mrs. George Bain. Here he met and immediately fell in love with Laura without giving any indication as to his attitude toward her. Strange, but for once Morrison seemed timid and afraid! He felt that surely so brilliant and superior a woman would never be willing to unite her fortune with so ordinary a person as himself, with the results that nearly two years passed before he was able to express his love to her. He wrote a number of letters, but did not mail them. He made several trips to Lexington with the explicit purpose of visiting her, but each time his heart failed and he left without seeing her. When he finally mustered courage to visit Miss Bain and tell her of his love he was accepted immediately. He then learned that from the first night she had seen him in the pulpit of the Hill Street Church, she had been saying to herself, "That's the man for me."

This marriage seemed to be all that such a union could be in love and mutual regard. Although married during the last months of Morrison's pastorate in Danville, their home was not really established until they moved into the parsonage in Frankfort the following fall. During the subsequent years three children were born: George Bain, Henry Clay, Jr., and Anna Laura.

The departure of the Morrisons from Danville in the fall of 1888 was almost as dramatic as had been his appointment a year earlier. In a Sunday evening service Morrison illustrated the difference between a willful sin and a mistake by telling of a housewife who unintentionally put too much soda in some biscuits. Although the family did not enjoy them, yet she had committed no sin. After a pause he remarked, "That good wife should not make that mistake too often."[15] Such frivolity in the pulpit was not pleasing to Colonel Proctor, who had been responsible for Morrison's call to the church, and he visited the pastor in his office the next morning. Seating himself he began the conversation by saying, "Brother Morrison, you know I let you have the money to go to Vanderbilt University." To which Morrison responded, "Yes, sir, and you know I paid every dollar of it back to you with six per cent interest." This was time for changing the subject. "Well, you know I came to the Conference, saw the Bishop, and secured your appointment to this place." Again the minister had a reply: "You may not have known there was a committee at the Conference asking for my appointment to a larger church than this." After a pause the conversation was resumed. "I came up here to say that if you want my endorsement, you must leave out some of the objectionable remarks that you make in your pulpit messages." The pastor's reply did not seem to be entirely satisfactory: "I will promise you to search for my text on my knees, but when I stand up to preach I am a free man without any promises to anybody. I sometimes say some things I regret, but my earnestness ought to be some atonement for my blunders." The Colonel made a few stammering remarks and left the office. Morrison says of that parting scene: "I followed him to the stairway and as he went down the stairs the bald spot on his head, about as large around as the top of a teacup, was very red. I could tell by the color of it that I would be removed from that church at the next Conference, and I was."[16]

At the conclusion of the Conference, which was held in Nicholasville in the fall of 1888, Bishop McTyeire, the same Bishop who a few years before had with prophetic vision sent H. C. Morrison to Stanford, now appointed him to Frankfort. This was the capital city, and had twice the population of Danville. The new appointment was considered to be one of the most influential pulpits in the Kentucky Conference. The prospects of preaching in its beautiful stone church and living in the comfortable brick parsonage did not detract from the desirability of the assignment. It was in his parsonage in Frankfort that Henry and Laura Morrison first "set up housekeeping. "

Two very busy but happy years were spent as minister to the Frankfort church. In spite of the spiritual lethargy of a congregation, which had not felt the power of an evangelistic awakening in years, three effective revivals were held during the period of Morrison's ministry. A large number of the worldly young people were converted and many of the members of long standing found that there was a difference between church membership and being "born again."

Opportunities for service outside the church were likewise presented to Morrison. During the Frankfort pastorate he served as chaplain for both the State Senate and the House of Representatives. His anxiety for the conversion of sinners frequently led him to preach in the Kentucky State Prison, located only a few blocks from the Methodist Church, and also to the passing throngs on the streets of the city. It was the large number of calls to assist in revival meetings in other churches, which made final his decision to give his full time to evangelism and the editing of a religious paper. As a result Henry Clay Morrison became known as an evangelist and an editor rather than as a pastor. Having risen in the pastorate to one of the best churches in his Conference he left that field of service in the fall of 1890, never to be regularly assigned to a pastorate again.

Notes

[1] *Some Chapters of My Life Story.*

[2] *The Pentecostal Herald.*

[3] *A Biographical Sketch of Henry Clay Morrison.*

[4] *Remarkable Conversions.*

[5] H. C. Morrison, "Diary," 1893, 1895-1910; 1913-41.

[6] *Some Chapters of My Life Story.*

[7] *Ibid.*

[8] *The Pentecostal Herald.*

[9] *Ibid.*

[10] *Ibid.*

[11] *Ibid.*

[12] *Ibid.*

[13] *Ibid.*

[14] *Some Chapters of My Life Story.*

[15] *Ibid.*

[16] *Ibid.*

Chapter 4
Publishing a Religious Paper

The romance of being an editor and publisher changes into an agonizing struggle when the visionary daydream is turned into reality. Without a sense of mission accompanied by a feeling of moral imperative the mortality rate of aspiring young editors would be high, or at least, so Henry Morrison felt while experiencing the many trials in the early years of publication of his own paper. It was only after a decade of struggle that he was able to arrive at a financial security, which enabled him to produce what was for years one of the most widely, read Bible-holiness papers.

The initial decision to edit such a paper came during his ministry in the Frankfort Methodist Episcopal Church, South. Even though he was actively engaged in pastoral work he received not less than twenty-five calls within a period of a few months from pastors within the bounds of the Kentucky and Louisville Conferences asking for his assistance in revival meetings. Many of these were from the larger churches of the area. The necessity of turning down these urgent appeals grieved him for he was painfully aware of the spiritual lethargy among the people. He felt that Kentucky Methodism had suffered untold injury because the use of the church altar as a place of public prayer, where sinners could seek forgiveness of sins, had been made a subject of ridicule by some of the church leaders. Many of the Methodist churches of central Kentucky had not witnessed a convert in years. "But worst of all," wrote Morrison, "there had arisen among us a small class of men, of considerable culture and influence, who claimed to be 'advanced thinkers', who seemed to hate the old Methodist doctrines worse than they did sin."[1] The only paper in the state making any claims to represent Methodism was the willing mouthpiece for this group. A large part of the lay membership of the church, however, did not follow this "liberal" leadership, but rallied around the old standards, with the result that revivals frequently broke out. The one great need was for a paper, which could combat false teachings and broadcast the Biblical truth of full salvation.

It was during a sleepless night in the fall of 1888, while holding a revival meeting in Maysville, Kentucky, that the burden of this situation struck Morrison. Of this experience he said: "As I lay there and thought and thought, my heart burned within me. I felt if I had the power to multiply myself into a score of men, I could make everyone of them an earnest preacher of the gospel."[2] It was then that it occurred to him to make use of the printed page: "At once the conviction seized me to publish a paper, call it 'The Old Methodist,' and with all my limited power advocate a return to the 'old paths' of Methodist doctrine and experience."[3] He felt this was a divine call, as clear to him as his call to preach. It was this sense of divine imperative, which kept Morrison closely associated with an editor's desk for his remaining fifty-three and a half years of life. Almost immediately after receiving this inspiration he rose from his bed, at about two o'clock, and wrote his first editorial. On the closing night of the revival he told the people of his plan to publish a four-page monthly paper, the purpose of which would be "to combat worldliness in the church, to lift up a standard against the teachers, of false and un-Methodistic doctrines, and to spread the doctrine of Christian holiness as taught by Paul and proclaimed by the founders of Methodism..."[4] Before he left, the people of Maysville gave him twenty-one subscriptions at fifty cents each.

Soon after his return to Frankfort, Morrison made arrangements with E. Polk Johnson, public printer and editor of *The Capital*, to print his new paper, *The Old Methodist*. Advertising was solicited from local merchants, and the first issue of five hundred copies was published about December 14, 1888. On Saturday evening after the first papers had been distributed, Morrison went to his room to check on finances, only to discover that the cost had been exactly fifteen dollars while the income from all sources had been only fourteen dollars and fifty cents. All the advertising space had been contracted and paid for several months in advance. The subscription money called for eleven more issues. He was fifty cents in the red on the first issue, and his financial resources were largely exhausted. The outlook seemed dark; for he had no personal funds with which to carry on the paper, yet he felt he had started the publication according to divine order. Furthermore, he now had a moral obligation to his subscribers and advertisers.

The following Sunday morning he went to his pulpit as usual and knelt behind the desk for prayer. He sought to look to the Lord for direction and help in the morning service, but as he prayed he constantly thought of that fifty-cent shortage. He was afraid to attempt to preach until he could get his mind off this financial problem, and as the minutes slipped by he became too ashamed to remain any longer on his knees. "Finally," he said, "I took a sort of mental running shoot and leaped out beyond the fifty cents and got a bit of help and assurance. I arose from my knees and went forward with the introductory service."[5]

From that time on he had a great deal more understanding and sympathy for the burdens carried by the businessmen of his congregations. Believing that faith without works is dead; Morrison sent sample copies of the paper to his friends throughout the state. Enough subscriptions were received to pay for the second issue. This greatly encouraged him, but even though the subscription list grew to about six hundred, the income was not sufficient to pay the expenses. At the close of nearly two years, when he left Frankfort, Morrison owed the printer three hundred dollars—a debt which was not paid for a number of months.

At the Annual Conference, which met in Lexington in September 1890, Morrison "located" in order that he might give his full time to evangelism and the publication of his paper. He moved both his papers and his family to Lexington. Office space, in which to carry forward the publishing interests, was rented on Main Street opposite the post office. A half-interest in the paper was sold to the Rev. C. F. Oney, who had that year been placed in charge of a mission in Lexington. The five hundred dollars received from this sale gave capital with which to enlarge the business. *The Old Methodist* was now changed from a monthly to a weekly and was continued as an eight-page paper. The name was also changed to *The Kentucky Methodist*. Enough type and other printer's supplies were now purchased to enable them to set up the paper in their own office. The forms were then hauled in a little pushcart to the Transylvania Publishing Company where the presswork was done.

Encouraging, as these improvements seemed, they did not bring an end to all the problems. Many church members did not take any religious paper and those who did were usually quite attached to the one, which had been coming into their home for years and thus had little desire to change. Furthermore, *The Kentucky Methodist* took a strong stand for the Wesleyan interpretation of the Scriptures on the subject of entire sanctification—a doctrine which had been largely ignored by the Methodist Church, South. The editorial policy also opposed such social sins as dancing, card playing, theatergoing, and horse racing. It also insisted that the use of church suppers and fairs, as a means of obtaining the necessary funds for the church budget, were out of harmony with the true spirit of Christian giving. By the time the supporters of these practices were subtracted from the prospective list of subscribers, only a small proportion of the Methodists were left. Among the brethren who agreed with the policies and teachings of *The Kentucky Methodist* only a few had faith enough in the enterprise to invest the dollar, which was by now the subscription price of the paper.

The two partners faced the difficult situation by applying themselves diligently to the task of increasing their subscriptions. After writing friends, sending out circulars and propositions, they would sit in their office and look across at the post office "with as much solicitude as a small country boy waiting in the spring of the year for the first goose egg."[6] When the mail came in they would cross the street full of hope only to return "soberly reflecting over the fact that the common run of people are very slow in their appreciation of a good thing."[7]

After about six months of this struggle Oney grew discouraged and sold his interest to T. H. Morris, a practical newspaperman. He soon persuaded Morrison that Louisville would be a better place for publication than Lexington, and such a move was made in the spring of 1891. Rooms were rented, at 412 South Third Street, from Converse and Company, publishers of *The Christian Observer,* a Presbyterian paper. Since the new offices were just above the pressrooms it was convenient to set up the paper and send the forms down to the presses.

This move to Louisville involved considerable expenditure of both time and money. Morrison felt it would be necessary to quit the evangelistic work for a time to get the paper established in its new location. The problem of support for his family was solved, however, by his call to serve as supply pastor in the Broadway Methodist Church in Louisville. The talented and popular pastor, Dr. Gilbey Kelley, had to be relieved of his duties because of poor health. Bishop Robert K. Hargrove asked the Rev. G. B. Overton, presiding elder of the Louisville District, to put H. C. Morrison in as supply until the Annual Conference. This was just the opportunity Morrison needed. The duties were limited to preaching in the regular Sunday services and conducting the mid-week prayer meeting. The salary of one hundred dollars a month was small, but adequate to meet the needs of the family. During this period of about six months, from April to September, Morrison was able to get the publication program fairly well organized. Although much effort was expended in trying to persuade him to accept the Broadway Church as a regular appointment, Morrison was firm in his decision to return to evangelistic work.

At this juncture another person became interested in *The Kentucky Methodist*. Morrison's long-time friend, H. B. Cockrill, inherited several hundred dollars from his father and proposed buying an interest in the paper. Soon after this purchase of a third interest in the paper, Morris grew discouraged over the financial prospects and sold his share to the other two men.

Subsequent to this transaction the publication of weekly articles from such well-known evangelists as Dr. Beverly Carradine, of St. Louis, and the Rev. T. H. B. Anderson, then located in California, stimulated wider interest in the paper. The distribution now spread to so many sections of the country that the name *Kentucky Methodist* was hardly appropriate, thus it was changed to *The Methodist*. Four years after Cockrill joined the business they bought out another holiness paper which the Rev. W. A. Dodge of Georgia had been publishing under the title *The Way of Life*. The combined lists boosted the number of subscriptions to fifteen thousand, and the paper now carried the caption *The Methodist* and *The Way of Life*. It continued under this name for two years.

During the period from 1880-1910 there was a great deal of controversy within Methodism over the Wesleyan interpretation of the scriptural doctrine of entire sanctification. There was an element within the Methodist Church, South which opposed those who advocated the doctrine of entire sanctification. Since Morrison was publishing one of the few papers in the Southland, which stood out strongly for this doctrine, he became the target of much criticism.

Chief among his critics was *The Central Methodist*, an official publication of Kentucky Methodism. Through its pages he was accused of desiring to split the church, planning to organize a new church out of the splinter, and getting himself appointed as Bishop. Morrison's frontal attack may not have been the wisest or most diplomatic method—his sincerity can scarcely be doubted. According to his own testimony he loved his church and had no desire whatsoever either to form a new organization or attain official position in either it or a new church. Southern Methodism had been his spiritual mother and his great desire was to revive the neglected doctrine of entire sanctification as he believed it had been taught by such eminent Methodists as John and Charles Wesley, John Fletcher, Richard Watson, Adam Clarke, and Bishops Francis Asbury and William McKendree. Apparently some of his relatives, the Bains in particular did not fully sympathize with the crusade he was making. When the postman brought the copies of *The Central Methodist*, his wife, Laura, would quickly examine them, and if they contained articles criticizing her husband, would burn them in order that her parents, with whom the Morrisons were living, "might not see what a disturber of peace they had for a son-in-law."[8]

During many months of accusation and misrepresentation, Morrison wrote only one editorial in his personal defense. Great credit for this attitude of restraint was due to the influence of Dr. W. P. Harvey, a Baptist minister who was at that time business manager of the Western Recorder, a Baptist periodical. On one occasion some men at the Annual Conference had given Morrison some data relative to one of his most bitter critics. The facts were of such nature that were they published, they would not only have silenced his criticism, but would likely have made necessary his moving from the state. On the way home from the Conference Morrison met Dr. Harvey on the train and showed him the information he had at hand. After examining the papers Dr. Harvey replied:

> No doubt if you publish these facts he will become silent. But don't do it Morrison. That is not your line; you are standing for a great religious experience. If you should publish the facts you have it would humiliate that man and, perhaps, destroy any usefulness he may have, and his family will have to suffer. That is not your line of battle. Pigeonhole that stuff, but do not publish it. Stick to your purpose to make a spiritual paper a blessing to your readers, and pay little attention to your critics.[9]

On the one occasion in which Morrison wrote in his defense he felt a rebuke of God's Spirit: "If you wish to take care of yourself I see no reason why I should be at pains to take care of you."[10]

The pecuniary problems of the publishing business continued for some years. In fact, Morrison declared that "for seven years after it was launched it did not earn a postage stamp above expenses."[11] The turning point, so far as financial matters are concerned, came as a result of a very unusual circumstance. Following a conflict which arose in connection with his having fulfilled a preaching engagement in a camp meeting in Dublin, Texas, in September 1896, Morrison was expelled from the ministry and membership of the Methodist Episcopal Church, South.[12] Although he was later completely exonerated, the incident attracted enough attention to greatly increase the number of subscriptions to *The Methodist* and *the Way of Life*. During the spring of 1897, as many as four hundred new subscriptions per day were coming in. The publicity, which was worth at least $10,000 by his estimate, enabled the paper to operate on a sound financial basis for the first time.

Morrison's periodical was destined to go through three more changes of name before coming to its present title. Until 1897 it continued as *The Methodist* and *The Way of Life*. With the growing opposition of the church to the teachings and work of its editor, this title was frequently criticized as indicating some official connection with Methodism. It was on August 11, 1897, that the first issue of the paper appeared bearing the name, *The Pentecostal Herald*. This made clear to everyone that the theological emphasis of the paper was to be upon the need of "an abiding Pentecost, of the presence and work of the Holy Spirit."[13] He refused to change the name even after modern "Pentecostalism" came to be largely associated with the speaking in an unknown tongue. "This name," he said, "was given to *The Herald*, and carried by it for many years before what is now know as the 'Tongues Movement', or a Pentecostal movement connected with speaking in tongues."[14] In 1932, *The Way of Faith*, a full-salvation paper, which has been published for many years in Columbia, South Carolina, was merged with

The Pentecostal Herald, and for the remainder of Morrison's life the paper bore the title, *The Pentecostal Herald* and *The Way of Faith*. Shortly after his death in 1942, the new editorial staff shortened the name to *The Herald*. The emphasis of the paper is indicated in the subtitle, "A Journal of Full Salvation and The Way of Faith."

For fourteen years after the publication interests were moved to Louisville the work was carried on in rented property. First it was the upstairs room at 412 South Third Street, then on Fourth Street between Main and the river, and finally it was moved to 317 West Walnut.

Beginning early in 1904, Morrison made an appeal for money with which to build what he termed his "Pentecostal Building." This was to house the printing plant and a large auditorium, which was to be used as a Full Gospel Mission along the lines of the Salvation Army program. Twenty thousand dollars was the goal set for the financial drive in this project. By June of that year $4,441 had been subscribed, and with this money a lot and an old Lutheran Church was purchased at 1821 West Walnut Street. The building had a seating capacity of about four hundred, but with some remodeling it could be made to accommodate one thousand. Nearly enough bricks were piled on the ground to build pressrooms. By 1907 its evaluation was $10,000, and it bore an indebtedness of only one thousand. The publishing interests continued to operate from this location until June, 1917, when the printing plant and editorial offices were moved to the present location, 523 South First Street.

One indication of good employer-employee relationship is a low rate of turnover among the workers. According to this standard the Pentecostal Publishing Company would rate high. Over a period of fifty years only three persons were dismissed, though some left voluntarily for positions that seemed to offer greater opportunity. The majority of the force remained with *The Herald* for twenty years or more. Only four men served as business manager during a period of sixty years; A. D. Hicks, W. E. Arnold, V. L. Williams, and J. H. Pritchard. It was in 1897 that Mr. J. H. Pritchard first became associated with the company. His being a nephew of Morrison may have increased his interest in the business, but whatever the reason, next to Morrison, more credit belongs to him for the success of the Pentecostal Publishing Company than to anyone else.

The editorial staff presents a very similar pattern as to terms of service. Several persons served as office editor for short periods: W. E. Arnold, John Paul, and C. F. Wimberly. Mrs. Elizabeth Whitehead joined *the Herald* staff on September 1, 1906. For several years she worked in the circulation department and aided the assistant editor. In 1911 she was elected assistant editor, which position she held until after her marriage to H. C. Morrison on February 17, 1916. Afterwards she was listed as the Associate Editor, which position she continued to fill until her death in 1945. It was she who actually carried on the editorial work throughout these years, for Morrison was away from the office most of the time.

Even with the best of office personnel few independent religious papers are able to long endure unless they champion some particular doctrine. There can be no doubt but that the doctrine of entire sanctification, as a second definite work of grace subsequent to regeneration, was the outstanding point emphasized by *The Pentecostal Herald*. The paper came into being during the great "holiness revival," which swept across America during the last two decades of the nineteenth century. Morrison felt that this doctrine was not only Biblical, but also that it had been the distinctive position of early Methodism. He considered it to be his mission to stress and, if possible, restore this teaching to the Methodist church. Later on, with the turn of the century, it became necessary to contend for the doctrine of regeneration—thousands having been received into the membership of the church without conviction of their sins or the knowledge of the regenerating power of Christ. After the influx of German rationalism during the second decade of the present century, the battle area was enlarged to include the defense of the Bible itself against the attacks of the "destructive critics." Other objectives in *The Herald's* spiritual crusade include an attack upon the movie industry, especially the use of movies in the church; the support of the temperance and prohibition movement; old-fashioned evangelism; and the doctrine of the premillennial coming of Christ.

One measure of the success of a periodical is the number of subscribers. One of the most successful promotional schemes was the special twenty-five cent offers by which the paper would be sent to a new subscriber during the last four or five months of the year for one-fourth of the yearly subscription rate. As examples of the success of these drives, in 1935, 22,000 and in 1941, 26,000 new subscriptions were received. The constant growth of the paper can be seen through such statistics as the following: beginning with 500 copies in the first issue the circulation grew to 15,000 in 1893, 30,000 in 1920, 38,000 in October, 1934, and 55,000 during the summer of 1942.[15] During the first fifty years more than sixty millions of copies of this paper were sent out to be read by millions of people. At least two persons, Mr. Alvin J. Overstreet of Wilmore, Kentucky, and Mrs. G. F. Byrd of Blossom, Texas, subscribed for the first number and had not missed an issue at the end of a half-century.

Still other evidences of the influences of the paper may be gleaned from testimonials. Even after making allowances for some exaggeration one's thought is stimulated by Morrison's statement that: "There is not a two-horse wagon bed in the state of Kentucky that would hold the letters that through the years have come to this office from people who have been converted, reclaimed, sanctified, or greatly helped through the reading of this paper." Dr. George B. Winton, editor of the St. Louis Christian is said to have listed *The Pentecostal Herald* as one of the two or three theologically conservative papers having an influence in the theological controversies which were agitating the General Conference of the Methodist Episcopal Church, South, in 1922.[16] Dr. J. W. Weldon in an address made at the Sesquicentennial celebration of Kentucky Methodism in 1933 stated: "I seriously doubt if there is another man in worldwide Methodism whose messages, week by week, reach more people and whose influence in promoting experimental religion is as great today as that of Dr. H. C. Morrison...."[17]

The scope of influence was enlarged when the Pentecostal Publishing Company expanded its activities beyond the weekly paper. W. E. Arnold was responsible for starting it in the book-publishing and book-selling business. The result was the printing and selling of several million copies of religious books. For a short time, about 1901-1906, they published a monthly Holiness magazine called *The Pentecostal Century*. For a period of more than three years (1903-07) the staff edited and published Pentecostal Sabbath-school literature. Although the circulation of this material was increasing in a very satisfactory manner, it was deemed best to transfer this work in 1907 to the Nazarene Publishing Company of Los Angeles, California. Here it became the basis for the Sunday school literature since published under the auspices of the Church of the Nazarene.

To one acquainted with the life and work of H .C. Morrison, even a suggestion that his paper would do anything but support the program of Christian education would be absurd. The many holiness colleges which arose with the growth of the holiness movement were advertised in the columns of

The Herald, and also received moral support from the editor's potent pen. Perhaps the best illustration of Morrison's desire to use *The Herald* for the advancement of the educational program can be seen in the fact that upon his death the Pentecostal Publishing Company was to be incorporated as "The Morrison Theological Trust" with all profits to be used for the benefit of such "educational institution or institutions as prepare for the ministry wholly sanctified young men...."[18]

In candor it must be said that Morrison was not a highly educated man, and his writings show the marks of the warrior rather than those of the scholar. Only a few days out of each year were spent in his office. His editorial desk consisted largely of tables in hotel rooms and worker's tents in camp meetings. In taking these factors into account the considerate fellow human will frankly recognize the weaknesses of Morrison's humanity, but will salute the achievements of one who was able to successfully found and edit an independent religious paper for more than half a century.

Notes

[1] *The Pentecostal Herald.*

[2] *Ibid.*

[3] *Ibid.*

[4] *Ibid.*

[5] *Ibid.*

[6] *Ibid.*

[7] *Ibid.*

[8] *Ibid.*

[9] *Ibid.*

[10] *Some Chapters of My Life Story.*

[11] *The Pentecostal Herald.*

[12] *Ibid.*

[13] *Ibid.*

[14] *Ibid.*

[15] H. C. Morrison, "Diary," 1893, 1895-1910; 1913-41.

[16] *The Pentecostal Herald.*

[17] *Ibid.*

[18] "Articles of Incorporation, The Morrison Theological Trust" (Louisville, Sept. 18, 1942).

Chapter 5
Twenty Years of Evangelism

At the time H. C. Morrison left the pastorate to enter the work of full-time evangelism, the Methodist church had no plans in its ecclesiastical organization for this type of Christian service. Since the Conference could not give an appointment to this work, it was necessary for Morrison to discontinue his membership. For the next twenty years he served as a local preacher engaged in full-time evangelism. The complete story of those years of activity, with their successes and disappointments, joys and heartbreaks will never be fully told.

Morrison related that one of the saddest days of his life was in September, 1890, when he stood up at the Kentucky Annual Conference, which met in Lexington, and asked that Bishop R. K. Hargrove give him local relationship in order that he might give his full time to evangelism.[1] The termination of his membership in the traveling connection of the Conference seemed like breaking the tie of a high and sacred fraternity.[2]

The feeling of loneliness, which resulted, was only intensified by the fact that he left the Conference having only one request to hold evangelistic services. This was difficult for Morrison to understand, since the year before, while still pastor of the Frankfort Church, he had received not less than thirty calls to hold revivals in churches within the bounds of the

Kentucky Conference. Apparently his brethren of "the cloth" either did not wish his services now that he was an evangelist, or else were so busy they had forgotten to speak to him before the close of the Conference. Although in the succeeding years he held revivals in large churches from coast to coast, he never received many invitations from central Kentucky.

The only meeting slated at the close of this conference was for the Rev. J. A. Sawyer, presiding elder in one of the mountain districts. He asked Morrison to hold his Quarterly Conference in Middlesboro and Pineville, Kentucky, and to preach for a week or ten days in each place. They were successful but not very remunerative meetings. Even though he had been disappointed at the conference, sufficient requests were received to fill his time for the next six months with scarcely an intermission. At the end of this period he was greatly fatigued and suffered with a sore throat because he had not yet learned how to conserve his strength. It was at the close of the revival in Hopkinsville, Kentucky, in which nearly one hundred members were added to the church, that he received an invitation to serve as supply pastor of the Broadway Church in Louisville.

This short interim pastorate not only afforded opportunity for the organization of Morrison's publishing interests, as has been previously noted, but likewise furnished time for physical rest before entering a period of almost continual evangelism extending through more than fifty years. Morrison introduced his first sermon in the Broadway Church by saying: "I believe that every great city church needs a preacher for a few months who would stay longer if he could, and could not stay longer if he would."[3] Now a man of thirty-four years he was described as:

> a brilliant young pastor...who, though not knowing it himself, was a born leader, as well as

an eloquent, forceful preacher. He had dark hair, a dropping mustache, and a unique round gray spot was beginning to form in the front of an impressive shock of hair that made him look like an artist. He was gaunt, graceful, and wiry, with a keen mind, a musical voice and a spirit that was independent to a degree most tantalizing to the old-line churchmen who believed in regularity and were opposed to being "righteous over much."[4]

Although it had been understood when he began his work with the Broadway Church that he was an evangelist, still, as the time for the 1891 Conference drew near, the presiding elder, the Rev. G. B. Overton, urged Morrison to accept an appointment. To this Morrison replied by saying, "Brother Overton, if a committee should come to me from Dr. [T. DeWitt] Talmage's Church in New York and should offer me $10,000 a year to take charge of that great church I should not consider it for a moment. I feel without a doubt that I am divinely called to the evangelistic work."[5] After a long pause Overton, with tears in his eyes, replied: "Morrison, I will never say another word to you about giving up your evangelistic work,"[6] and he never did. So far as available records indicate this was the last instance of Morrison's serving in any sort of pastoral relationship.

The next three years were a time of busy evangelism. Dr. T. H. B. Anderson invited him to assist in revival meetings in the Methodist Episcopal Church, South, in Sacramento, California. Thus began what was to be a long though intermittent evangelistic ministry on the West Coast—a ministry which was to result not only in spiritual blessing for many, but was also to be of inestimable value to Asbury College and Asbury Theological Seminary.

At least one experience came to Morrison on his way to California, which had such an influence upon his subsequent ministry that it is worth recording here. On his westward journey he stopped to assist in a revival meeting in a little Texas town where a Rev. Mr. Lively was pastor. While there, Morrison received a letter from Dr. Anderson canceling the meeting in Sacramento because the opposition to the preaching of holiness would make his coming at that time unwise. Having either canceled or refused to accept invitations to conduct revivals farther east, he was now far from home with few if any prospect for meetings. The outlook was dark. It seemed as though every door was closing against him. Under this burden Morrison went, morning after morning, into a pine woods to pray. One morning, he related, the Holy Spirit answered his prayer by giving to him the promise; "Behold, I have set before thee an open door, and no man can shut it." Whenever times of opposition or discouragement came throughout the remainder of his life, Morrison would present this to God as a promise, which He was bound to keep.

The first four and a half months of 1895 were spent in revival work in California. During this time campaigns were conducted in Sacramento, Woodland, Winters, San Francisco, Oakland, Coverdale, and Los Angeles. It was on January 6, in the course of the meeting in Sacramento, that he met Mrs. Elizabeth Glide, who was later to become a great benefactress to Asbury College. While in California, Morrison reported that he preached one hundred and ninety times with the result that one hundred and seventy claimed the experience of entire sanctification, in addition to a large number who professed to be either reclaimed from a backslidden state or to have received forgiveness of sins for the first time.

The next ten years constituted for Morrison a period of strenuous labor, combined with severe trials. The closing decades of the nineteenth century were times of bitter opposition on the part of many in Methodist ecclesiastical authority to those who advocated the doctrine of entire sanctification or heart holiness.[7] In 1898 the General Conference passed legislation giving to local pastors authority to prohibit evangelists from holding meetings within the territory surrounding their churches. As a result, Morrison withdrew his membership from the Methodist Church during the fall of that same year in order to avoid breaking an ecclesiastical law while conducting meetings in Terrell, Texas.

Many of the laymen of the Church, as well as some of those in ecclesiastical authority, felt no personal animosity toward Morrison, as is manifested by the honors and responsibilities which they placed upon him during those first twenty years of his evangelistic ministry. Since he was no longer a clerical member of the Annual Conference, he was chosen by the district as a lay delegate in 1901.[8] In that same Conference he was elected as a lay delegate to the General Conference of the Methodist Episcopal Church, South, which met in Dallas, Texas, in the spring of 1902. Four years later he was elected alternate lay delegate to the General Conference. He also was asked to be one of the special speakers for the Pentecostal meetings held in connection with the General Conference of the Methodist Episcopal Church, in Los Angeles, in 1904, and again in Baltimore, Maryland, in 1908. Throughout the two decades under consideration (1890-1910), Morrison preached in nine different Annual Conferences of either the Northern or the Southern branch of the Methodist Church. These testimonials of confidence helped greatly to compensate for the severe criticism and persecution, which others had caused him to endure.

At no time during his ministry did Morrison become what some have termed a "commercial evangelist." His oratorical ability made it possible for him to rise to pinnacles of greatness while preaching to crowds that were numbered by the thousands, yet he never saw fit to organize an evangelistic party with a business manager and an advance press agent for the purpose of conducting city-wide revival campaigns. Instead, he filled his slate year after year with meetings in individual churches where the converts would be left in a church home, under the care of the pastor.

The use of this method does not imply that his was not a well-organized and carefully conducted program. For nearly thirty years his plan called for three preaching services on the opening Sunday-the afternoon service being for men only. By this method he hoped to interest the men of the church who would in turn bring their families and friends to the services. Morrison usually preached twice each weekday with the exception of Saturday, which he set aside as a rest day. Early in each campaign he planned to contact the leaders of the various church organizations, getting the membership to visit the delinquents and do personal work among the unsaved. Special days of prayer were announced. One thing he could not tolerate was a disorderly service. To prevent confusion caused by visiting among friends, he sought to take charge ten minutes before the hour announced for the beginning of the service. Having himself found Christ at an altar of prayer, he believed absolutely in this time-honored method and used it whether preaching in the fastidious city church or a brush-arbor camp meeting. To the average congregation his sermon was the high point of the service.

> His masterful sermons, and kind, brotherly, loving heart won the people who heard him gladly. Many pressed their way to the altar for pardon and cleansing, and shouts of victory rent the air; the prejudice and formality were broken

up and the tide rose to the close of the meeting, which was run on the trunk line of fun salvation from start to finish. The preacher clothed full salvation in its best dress. His sermons were like poetry in prose, rippling with rhetoric, like a running brook. He doesn't weary the audience with long drawn arguments, but buttresses his sermons with "Thus saith the Lord," which is stronger than logic. His fund of original illustrations is inexhaustible. He hangs the galleries with pictures of exquisite beauty, entrancing his audience, while he shells them with heavy artillery of truth. He is unanswerable and people do not attempt to talk back to him. He fights and conquers with love. Back of his masterful sermons people see a brother with a heart overflowing with love. He grapples for the lowest sinner. Like his Master, he is in a pre-eminent sense, "the friend of sinners."[9]

The fact that Morrison did not hold union, citywide revival campaigns should not be construed to mean that he was not a busy and successful evangelist. For a period of sixteen years in which fairly accurate statistics are available it has been determined that he participated in more than twenty campaigns per year. During this period he conducted meetings in thirty-six states, the District of Columbia, Canada, Cuba, Palestine, Egypt, India, Burma, Philippine Islands, China, Korea, and Japan. Kentucky headed the list with sixty-six meetings, followed by Texas, California, Tennessee, Ohio, and Mississippi with fifteen or more each. Ten states are listed in which only one Morrison revival campaign was conducted. During the one year, 1906, he preached in five different colleges and "saw about six hundred students either converted or sanctified."[10] A note in Morrison's "Diary" under the date December 31, 1908, indicated that he preached four hundred seventy-one times that year. A list of twenty-six meetings showed a total of 1,723 people who received the grace of either conversion or entire sanctification.

Additional statistics would neither add nor detract greatly from an evaluation of Morrison's work during those years, but having already related something of the bitter opposition, which he faced, it would seem only fair to relate some favorable reactions. In one meeting in Franklin, Tennessee, the crowd was so large that Morrison had to climb in a rear window in order to get to the platform of the church. In Greensburg, Kentucky, every store in town was closed and the public school was dismissed in order that the people might attend the revival meeting.

A particular role in which Morrison became very well known was that of a camp meeting preacher. The two decades—1890 to 1910—presented the period of greatest activity in the development of the holiness camp meeting movement. As a result of the holiness revival within the Protestant denominations, large numbers were led to profess the experience of entire sanctification. During this period there was growing opposition, on the part of those in ecclesiastical authority, toward the "second blessing" folks. The holiness camp meetings were organized prior to the rise of the "holiness churches," which provided new church homes for many who professed this experience. These camp meetings furnished not only a means for evangelizing those as yet untouched by the message of holiness, but also as a place where spiritual sustenance could be obtained by those who professed to be in possession of this grace.[11] Morrison became one of the most widely known of the camp meeting preachers. During the period from 1893 to 1910 he was engaged as a special speaker in nearly one hundred camp meetings by more than sixty different camp meeting organizations.

The life of the camp meeting preacher was not an easy one. Many of the camps were newly organized and few facilities were provided for the comforts of the workers. Morrison was a preacher in the first season for the Peniel Camp located near Greenville, Texas. The following is a description of the accommodations provided:

> Wife and I stayed in a tent. It was pointed out to us as being ready for us. The floor was the bare ground; there was a plank about ten feet long and ten inches wide with a wash pan, a tin bucket, and a towel; a bale of hay with a sheet and two quilts. Those were the furnishings. I got some nails and drove in one of the tent stakes [poles], which served as our hat rack and wardrobe. I hunted up a couple of short planks, drove some stakes in the ground to support them, cut open my bale of hay, spread between these planks and tucked one of the quilts in to hold the hay together. Someone brought us a couple of pillows, and we made ourselves very comfortable.[12]

Many of the camps were located in isolated spots so far as travel facilities were concerned. Often in order to reach the next appointment it was necessary to leave one camp in the middle of the night and drive with a horse and wagon until daybreak in order to catch an early morning train.

One may wonder about Morrison's personal and family life during those years of assiduous evangelism. The picture is filled with both sunshine and shadow. When the Morrisons left the parsonage at Frankfort in September 1890, they had no home of their own into which to move. At the invitation of Mr. and Mrs. George Bain, the Morrison family went to live with them in Lexington. Since both Colonel Bain and Morrison were away almost constantly on lecture tours and revival meetings, the privilege of companionship was mutually enjoyed by both mother and daughter for a period of three years.

The fall of 1893 was one never to be forgotten by Henry Morrison. For what must have seemed like a fleeting moment, the Morrisons enjoyed the pleasure of living in their own home in Lexington. On September 25 a down payment of $138.13 closed the deal on a purchase of a little $2,700 cottage. The next day they moved into their little home. The thrill of that experience was short-lived however, for on October 1 Morrison was away again to begin a series of revival meetings. From then until November 10 when he left for New Orleans, he was privileged to spend just seven days at home.

It was on Saturday, November 25, while still engaged in a revival meeting in New Orleans, that Morrison received a telegram stating that his wife was ill. As he awaited the first train going north, a second telegram came telling that she was dying. It was the next evening at eight o'clock when he finally arrived at her bedside and found that "she was calm, sweet, full of faith, resigned and going down to death."[13] She lingered for several days, death finally claiming her at 8:10 Wednesday evening, November 29, 1893.

The funeral service was conducted the following Sunday afternoon in the home of her parents, Colonel and Mrs. Bain. The sustaining power of God in the hours of deep sorrow can be seen through Morrison's testimony on this sad day when he said: "I do not seem to need the comfort the preacher would give me. I rest in the Lord today... It snows but the grave has lost its horror. She is in heaven. I cannot feel that she is in the grave."[14]

The day after the funeral the little cottage in Lexington was sold to Colonel Bain. The three little children, George Bain, Henry Clay, Jr., and Anna Laura were left, as their father had once been, to be cared for by the loving hands of their grandparents. Taking leave from his children and from Mr. and Mrs. Bain, Morrison left to resume the evangelistic work to which God had called him.

More than a year of active crusading against sin and unrighteousness had transpired since the sorrow of death had destroyed the happy home of Henry Morrison, when, as he was conducting the second of his California revival meetings, a union meeting held in Woodland in February 1895, he felt the stir of a new romance. Some time before, Miss Geneva Pedlar, whose home was in San Francisco, had attended a holiness camp meeting where she was sanctified wholly. While visiting in Woodland, California, where she had lived as a girl, her former Sunday School teacher took her to the revival meeting which was being conducted by Henry Morrison. This meeting resulted in their marriage a few weeks later. The wedding took place at eight o'clock in the evening on April 9, 1895, in the Grace Methodist Episcopal Church in San Francisco.[15]

Following a short honeymoon trip to the beautiful little village of Sausalito, up the bay from San Francisco, Henry Morrison and his twenty-year-old bride went to Cloverdale, California, where they began another revival meeting. During the first three years of their marriage, Geneva traveled almost constantly assisting him in the revival work. Her husband testified that "She had a remarkable magnetism and gave a beautiful testimony, and frequently delivered telling messages."[16]

It was in the fall of the same year that the Morrison's purchased a lot and began the construction of a cottage at O'Bannon, a village on the outskirts of Louisville, Kentucky. Here their first two children were born-Howard on March 14, 1898, and Geneva, on February 4, 1900.

Some of the usual enjoyments of home life, necessarily sacrificed by the evangelist, may be seen through recounting experiences of the Morrisons. On May 8, 1901, Mrs. Morrison boarded a train with her two small children, making the long trip to San Francisco without the assistance of her husband. While visiting her parents there she gave birth to a second son, Franklin Durham, on August 3, 1901. The father, Henry Morrison, did not have the privilege of seeing his wife and family from the time of their parting in May until October 12.

A little more than two years later the experience was repeated, with only a slight variation. On February 7, 1904, Mrs. Morrison and the children took the train from St. Louis to San Francisco and Geneva did not see her husband again until she and their oldest son, Howard, went down to Los Angeles on April 9 to rejoin him in evangelistic work there. On April 24, 1904, their second daughter, Emily, was born in the Deaconess hospital in Los Angeles. By June 6 Mrs. Morrison was back in San Francisco, staying with her parents, while her husband was once more away keeping his evangelist schedule. They were not to see each other again until she and the family joined him on October 25 while he was engaged in revival meetings in Selma, California. The next three months were spent in Los Angeles, where they rented a house for the winter since Morrison's meetings were held in the vicinity; thus he was able to keep in close touch with the family, especially during the time that his wife was in the hospital and later while she was recuperating from the effects of major surgery. With the coming of spring, he was once again away to fill his heavy schedule of revival and camp meeting engagements.[17]

Morrison's youngest daughter, Helen, was born in Wilmore, Kentucky, on March 10, 1910. Her father had left nearly seven months before on a world tour of evangelism, and was preaching in the orient at the time of her birth. In this day of "G. I. wives," such situations are common and little thought of, but fifty-odd years ago the absence of a husband on a tour, which would take him away from the shores of the homeland at such a time was so unusual that it furnished the topic of conversation among many of the women of Wilmore, Kentucky, the little village in which the Morrisons were living at the time. Thus even as the clouds pass across the sunlit sky throwing their shadows upon the objects below, so the entrancing life of the evangelist was accompanied by its crosses.

Morrison's interest in missions became manifest during this period of his life. Once having caught this vision, evangelical, evangelistic Christianity and the support of worldwide missions seemed to him to be inseparable. During the first decade of the present century Morrison's missionary interest manifested itself through his leadership in the organization of the Pentecostal Church in Cuba, and in his world tour of evangelism.

The Spanish-American War easily aroused the militant spirit of H. C. Morrison to a spiritual crusade against the sin and wickedness that had been prevalent in those lands, which were taken over from Spain by the United States. As early as December of 1898, articles began to appear in *The Herald* urging the sending of missionaries to Cuba. Morrison lent his whole-hearted support to this program and soon the Pentecostal Publishing Company was acting as treasurer for such funds.

Active missionary work was started in March 1900, when Morrison made his first trip to Cuba. The mission enterprise so prospered that on December 14, 1903 the Pentecostal Christian Church was organized with about one hundred seventy-five members. The Pentecostal Mission in Cuba was started as something definitely outside of, and distinct from, any enterprise sponsored by the Methodist Church. Morrison felt that the same ecclesiastical leaders who had opposed holiness evangelism and holiness camp meetings were just as much opposed to the spread of the same teachings on the mission field. He vehemently rejected any suggestion that the Mission be given any denominational connection, and it continued as an independent enterprise for several years.

The story of the Cuba Mission cannot be completed without making reference to the Holiness Union of the South. For some time there had been agitation for an organization of the holiness forces of the South in a manner similar to the "National Association for the Promotion of Holiness" in the North. Their organizing convention held in Memphis, Tennessee, in October 1904, was followed in successive years by other annual conventions until at least 1912. Morrison was one of the leaders throughout the life of this organization. In 1906 they assumed the support of the Pentecostal Mission in Cuba. They continued to finance the church there until January 1, 1908, at which time, apparently with the blessing of Morrison, the church in Cardenas was accepted by the Methodist Conference. Morrison's interests seem to have been entirely diverted to other fields of activity.

The missionary emphasis of the Holiness Union became more evangelistic with each passing year. In the Birmingham convention in the fall of 1908 it was agreed that all direct missionary work of the Union should be evangelistic, assistance being given to movements that were already operating. It was in harmony with this trend that upon Morrison's receiving an invitation to be the speaker at the annual spiritual life conference in Lucknow, India, the Holiness Union voted to send him as their representative on a World Tour of Evangelism. The Union raised money to pay his expenses and also to pay one hundred dollars per month toward the support of his family.

Morrison filled the major portion of his camp meeting engagements for the summer of 1909, closing with the camp in Mooers, New York, on August 15. Mrs. Morrison and their four children accompanied him to this meeting in order to be together as long as possible before his departure on a world tour. Before leaving the campground Morrison took each of his children one by one into a thicket on the riverbank and had prayer with them. "We wept together and they promised if we meet no more on earth to meet me in heaven."[18] The emotional strain can be seen by another expression found in his diary: "Precious little children. My Father in heaven protects them. It seemed the biggest task of my life to say goodbye to wife and little ones."[19]

Henry Morrison and J. L. Piercy, an Asbury College student who was Morrison's traveling companion on this tour, boarded the ship in Montreal, Canada, on the evening of August 20 for a tour, which was to extend over a period of ten months. After brief visits to Scotland and England they spent a few days preaching in Port Said, Egypt, and nearly a week in Jerusalem. Three months were spent in intensive evangelism in India. In spite of the warm weather Morrison frequently spoke two and three times each day. He spoke before three Annual Conferences as well as other groups of Christian workers and revival services in the churches. While in Lucknow he stayed with E. Stanley Jones, who was pastor of a church in that city. Resolutions of appreciation for his services were passed by the Northwest India Conference, and the North Indian Conference, and many letters from individuals were mailed to him indicating the spiritual benefits which had been received. In all, the two evangelists traveled nearly six thousand miles in India before extending their tour into Burma and Singapore.

Their arrival in Hong Kong appeared next on the record of their travels. No sooner had they arrived there, however, than they received a cable from Bishop W. F. Oldham asking Morrison to come to Manila to conduct evangelistic services there in conjunction with the Annual Conference. These services were greatly blessed of the Lord, with many seeking for either pardon for sins or heart cleansing. So great was the effect that Bishop Oldham wrote to Morrison:

> But believe me, these men have received a spiritual uplift and revival impulse which promises to make an amazing difference in the future. When I cabled you, I did not know how marked a step forward your coming would bring... Your coming has practically impressed holiness as the birthright of every man in the Methodist Church, and I desire these revival bands to move through the country not only for the sake of sinners, but that we might have sincere saints. I think you may confidently look for five thousand professions of faith as a result of this revival campaign.[20]

Leaving Manila, Morrison and Piercy went to China on to Korea, where nearly thirty of the Korean preachers testified to having received the sanctifying grace. Services were held in the Wanamaker Y.M.C.A. hall in Seoul. "The crowds were so large they had to issue tickets of admission and the altars were filled, both by seeking pardon and Christians seeking sanctifying grace."[21] A final month in Japan concluded the evangelistic efforts enabling the two men to turn their faces toward home early in June 1910.

It was with a sense of relief that Morrison embarked for the trip across the Pacific. His health had been poor during most of the tour. He was tired when he reached India. There the heavy schedule of two and three services each day was enough in that hot climate to weaken even a strong man. In this weakened condition he was attacked by one of the worst types of dysentery germs in Asia. While being given a physical examination by a doctor in Manila, Morrison remarked: "Well, Dr., I will get rid of them, will I not?" To which the doctor replied, "I don't know, usually they get rid of the fellow."[22] At times he was so sick that he almost despaired of life. A diary entry says, "I have a feeling that I may not get out of India. Amen. It would be sweet to lie down and enter into rest. It would be wonderfully blessed to see my Lord."[23] According to Morrison's account it took a divine touch to give strength enough to continue the tour. He got on the boat at Manila too weak and sick even to eat. One night during the crossing from the Philippines to China he tells of having a vision of Jesus and Satan standing in his room talking about him. Satan was telling all about Morrison, "and every word of it was true." Finally, Jesus answered and said, "Satan, every thing you have said about Morrison is absolutely true, but he is one of my servants and he loves me with all his heart." With this both Satan and Jesus vanished, but the next morning Morrison awakened so much strengthened that he went to the dining room and ate a hearty breakfast. Even though he was to continue his work through China, Korea, and Japan his physical strength was largely depleted, and he needed greatly the rest afforded by the quiet trip across the Pacific toward the coast of California. Little did he realize that within a few months a call was to come which would close an epoch of full-time evangelism and place upon his shoulders a further responsibility—the presidency of Asbury College.

Notes

[1] *Some Chapters of My Life Story.*

[2] *The Pentecostal Herald.*

[3] *Ibid.*

[4] *Ibid.*

[5] *Some Chapters of My Life Story.*

[6] *Ibid.*

[7] Percival A. Wesche, "The Revival of the Camp Meeting by the Holiness Groups" (Unpublished M.A. Thesis, U. of Chicago, 1945). Hereafter referred to as "The Revival of the Camp Meeting by the Holiness Groups."

[8] *The Pentecostal Herald.*

[9] *Ibid.*

[10] *Ibid.*

[11] "The Revival of the Camp Meeting by the Holiness Groups."

[12] *The Pentecostal Herald.*

[13] *Ibid.*

[14] H. C. Morrison, "Diary," 1893, 1895-1910; 1913-41.

[15] *Ibid.*

[16] *Some Chapters of My Life Story.*

[17] H. C. Morrison, "Diary," 1893, 1895-1910; 1913-41.

[18] *Ibid.*

[19] *Ibid.*

[20] *Some Chapters of My Life Story.*

[21] *Ibid.*

[22] Letter from H. C. Morrison written to John Paul from Shanghai, China, March 16, 1910.

[23] H. C. Morrison, "Diary," 1893, 1895-1910; 1913-41.

Chapter 6
In Trouble with the Methodist Church

Reference has already been made to the conflict, which arose within Methodism during the closing years of the 19th century as a result of the "holiness revival," and to the opposition to holiness evangelists as evidenced by the activities of ecclesiastical leaders. A more elaborate discussion should be given to this situation as it resolved, in part, into a personal attack upon Henry Clay Morrison as one of the leaders in the holiness movement. The struggle between Morrison and the more liberal leaders focalized around three meetings: Dublin, Terrell, and Denton, Texas.

In the summer of 1895 several persons from Dublin attended the camp meeting at Waco, Texas, where they heard H. C. Morrison proclaim the doctrine of entire sanctification. After returning home they conceived the idea or holding a camp meeting in Dublin with Morrison as the evangelist. Early the following spring three laymen, one a member of the Methodist Episcopal Church, and the other two members of the Methodist Episcopal Church, South, wrote Morrison asking him to hold such a meeting in the Dublin city park. Inasmuch as many of the holiness camp meetings were sponsored by laymen, and not knowing of any opposition, he agreed to stop on his way to

California in September 1896, in compliance with their request. In July, the Rev. W. H. Matthews, preacher in charge of Dublin Station Methodist Episcopal Church, South, wrote Morrison requesting him not to come, and insisting that he take no part in meetings announced to be held in the city park. Whereas this was a period when many wild reports concerning the activities of holiness evangelists were circulated for the purpose of damaging their influence, Morrison thought this was just another such instance. Previous experiences had shown that many pastors, frightened by stories of radicalism, were soon won to supporting the revival once they heard the earnest, Biblical preaching of the evangelist. Consequently, he replied in a kindly manner, but insisted on going to fulfill his engagement.

Subsequent to this correspondence Morrison received a letter from the Rev. E. A. Smith, Presiding Elder of the Dublin District of the Northwest Texas Conference, threatening to test the ecclesiastical law relating to local preachers if the evangelist insisted upon coming. Morrison felt certain that he would be violating no law, but, due to the opposition, which had developed, asked the sponsors of the meeting for some further expression of community interest regarding their invitation. In response he received a petition, signed by the mayor of the city and 230 of the citizens requesting him to conduct the meeting in their midst. With this affirmation of widespread desire for his services he and another evangelist, the Rev. R. L. Averill, opened the tent-meeting in Dublin on September 4, 1896.

The following morning the Presiding Elder and the Pastor visited Morrison and asked him to leave the camp meeting. Since the warning produced no result they returned two days later to inform Morrison that charges were being preferred against him. He was invited to attend the committee meeting of local preachers and present any defense he might have, but Morrison was too busy with the revival services to attend any of the numerous sessions which were held for the purpose of drawing up charges and taking depositions against him. At the time the committee was in session twenty-five souls were either converted or sanctified. "The amusing feature about it all," according to Morrison, "was that the wife of one of the local preachers came to the tent while the committee was at work, and while her husband was preparing charges, she was most gloriously sanctified. She shouted and testified with great joy."[1]

On September 8, Morrison received a note from the Presiding Elder stating that he had suspended Morrison from the ministry of the Methodist Episcopal Church, South. The news of this opposition served as an advertisement. The people came in such throngs that they could not be seated in the tent and many stood outside in order to hear the sermons. More than 160 persons were either converted or sanctified under the ministry of Morrison and Averill in this campaign. Shortly before the close of the camp meeting Morrison was handed a copy or the charges and specifications, which had been forwarded to the Presiding Elder of the Lexington District. At this time Morrison held his membership in the Hill Street Methodist Church in Lexington, Kentucky, hence was subject to the jurisdiction of the officials there. While the Rev. Mr. Matthews and his associates had been thus engaged, a committee of prominent laymen from three or four of the Dublin churches was at work arranging to secure grounds for a holiness camp meeting to be held the following year.

Morrison forwarded the copies of charges and specifications to his friends, H. B. Cockrill and W. E. Arnold, who were asked to represent him in any trial, which might be held. He then continued with his original evangelistic itinerary on the West Coast. This kept him away from Kentucky until the latter part of February 1897. At the time he was tried by the

Quarterly Conference of the Hill Street Church in Lexington, Morrison was engaged in a revival campaign in St. James Methodist Episcopal Church in Denver, Colorado.

Morrison's prolonged absence did not prevent much public discussion of the coming trial. H. B. Cockrill presented views through the editorial columns of *The Methodist* published on November 18, 1896. The Rev. W. T. Bolling, Pastor of Hill Street Church, answered this article and defended his own part in the case, through the pages of *The Central Methodist*. He took the position that having received written complaints from the brethren in Texas the only course open to him was to appoint an investigating committee in harmony with paragraph 282 of the Discipline. This committee judged that Morrison had broken the law of the church through his disregard of the authority of the Presiding Elder of the Dublin District; consequently, the only course of action remaining was to refer the matter to the Quarterly Conference.

The Quarterly Conference of the Hill Street Methodist Episcopal Church, South, of Lexington, Kentucky, met on December 26, 1896, with the Rev. John Reeves, Presiding Elder, officiating. A layman from Waco, Texas, presented the case against H. C. Morrison. No accusation was made which involved either his character or the teaching of any heretical doctrine. The only charge was that of contumacious conduct, or failure to obey his superiors in office. The Conference was convinced that Morrison's actions in refusing to obey the Presiding Elder in Texas had violated a law of the church and thus he was guilty as accused. The Presiding Elder, John Reeves, then pronounced the sentence, which expelled Morrison from both the ministry and membership of the Methodist Episcopal Church, South.

It is interesting to note that some years later when the Rev. U. G. Foote became pastor of the Hill Street Church he was able to find no official record of Morrison's trial by the

Quarterly Conference of December 1896. It may be that it was expunged from the records at the request of the Annual Conference, or it may have been destroyed by the officials of the church in order that there would be no permanent record of an incident which proved to be unpleasant for all concerned. Whatever the attitude of the local church leaders may have been, it is interesting to note that Morrison was never asked to conduct another revival meeting in that church and it was a number of years before he was even invited to address its congregation.

The fact that the case was appealed to the Annual Conference indicates that there was a great deal of uncertainty over the legal aspects of the Morrison trial. There were wide differences of opinion as to just how paragraphs 109, 110, and 120 of the *Discipline* should be interpreted. It was not certain as to whether these statements gave jurisdiction to the Presiding Elder and local church pastor to control services held by other Methodist ministers "within the bounds" of the Methodist church, or whether such authority pertained only to services held in the churches of the charge. Since Morrison was not preaching in the Methodist Church in Dublin, Texas, but rather in the city park he maintained that he had violated no law of the church. This conclusion was validated by the subsequent decision of the Kentucky Annual Conference.

Morrison had not preached in a Southern Methodist Church for some time prior to his expulsion from the ministry on September 8, 1896, and refrained from doing so until after his restoration a year later. This procedure may have been necessitated in part by lack of calls from his Southern Methodist brethren, though it may also have been the desire to keep the letter of the law by not preaching in the pulpits of the church while being expelled from its ministry. These were not idle months, however, for Morrison received the sympathetic support of many church leaders. Dr. T. T. Eaton, pastor of Walnut Street Baptist Church in Louisville, and editor of *The Western Recorder*, wrote a very able editorial in defense of his Methodist friend. The Presiding Elder of the Louisville District of the Methodist Episcopal Church welcomed him to the pulpits of that district. Bishop Charles C. McCabe asked Morrison to join the Methodist Episcopal Church and assured him that he would have no opposition to the preaching of holiness. The sympathetic reaction to the action of the Methodist Episcopal Church, South, in having expelled Morrison without placing any accusations against either his character or his teaching was so great that it not only extended the field of evangelistic service, but greatly increased the number of subscriptions to his paper, *The Methodist* and *The Way of Life*.

The Kentucky Annual Conference of the Methodist Episcopal Church, South, held in Mt. Sterling, September 15-20, 1897, attracted much attention due to the struggle, which was anticipated in the disposition of the now celebrated "Morrison Case." The fact that John Reeves, the Presiding Elder who pronounced the sentence expelling Morrison, would likely be placed on trial did not diminish the excitement. When the vote was taken for Conference Secretary, Reeves, who had held office for some time, was defeated by W. F. Pollitt through a vote of fifty-eight to forty-eight. One of the members of the Conference said: "This vote is indicative of the sentiment in the Morrison-Reeve Case."[2]

The first day of the Conference brought charges and counter charges. As John Reeves reported the work of the Lexington District he announced the trial and expulsion of H. C. Morrison, local Elder, and also his appeal. He also challenged the legality of the appeal on the ground that Morrison had continued to preach even after he had been deprived of his ministerial credentials (though as noted above he had not done so in Southern Methodist Churches). In order to eliminate the possibility of Morrison having no other recourse to what he felt would be justice should the appeal be denied, W. E. Arnold, acting as attorney for Morrison, made complaints against John Reeves of maladministration of the trial by the Quarterly Conference. The Rev. W. T. Rowland also impeached the character of Reeves for violating the law of pro-rata. The objective of these brethren seemed not to have been to punish Reeves but to restore Morrison to his former place in the church. The conviction of Reeves appeared necessary to void the action of the Quarterly Conference over which he presided. "The Bishop ruled that the charge of maladministration should be read first, because if it as preferred be sustained there would be no case to appeal."[3]

The case dragged throughout the entire session of the conference. After a great deal of testimony had been presented by both sides, Bishop A. W. Wilson announced "that the proceedings in the case of H. C. Morrison's trial [at the Quarterly Conference] were vitally defective, and no trial has been had, and he stands where he did before the quarterly conference began trial." He also announced that the charge of maladministration against John Reeves had been withdrawn.[4] This pronouncement left Morrison under the suspension which had been imposed before the Quarterly Conference trial by the Rev. E. A. Smith, Presiding Elder of the Dublin District, and sustained by a committee of the Hill Street Church. All parties now worked toward a compromise settlement. Dr. Bolling, former pastor of Hill Street Church, went so far as to go to Lexington and hunt the committee which had said a trial was necessary and asked them to withdraw the charges. Morrison, on the other hand, prepared a statement, which he agreed should be read before the Annual Conference:

> I do not believe I was violating law when I held the Dublin meeting.
>
> I did not intend contumacious conduct by continuing to preach after my suspension.
>
> I never intended defiance of church law.
>
> If restored to its membership and ministry I will remain loyal to the church and obedient to its discipline while I continue in its connection.
>
> I am willing to make this statement before the Investigating Committee.[5]

With this statement Morrison was restored by the Bishop to his former position in the church and the case was closed. Official records of the trial before the Annual Conference cannot be obtained for a motion was passed by the Conference "to expunge from the minutes all the testimony, oral and written," and "the Secretary was instructed to enter in the minutes the fact of the charge and that satisfactory adjustment had been made."[6]

One of the sequels to this affair was the insertion of paragraph 30 into the *Discipline* of the Southern Methodist Church, by the General Conference of 1898. It read:

> Any traveling or local preacher or layman, who shall hold public religious services within the bounds of any mission, circuit or station, when requested by the preacher in charge not to hold such services, shall be deemed guilty of imprudent conduct, and shall be dealt with as the law provides in such cases.[7]

One of the problems related to this new law was the interpretation of the term "within the bounds of." This could be so construed as to give a pastor the right to govern the preaching activities of any member of the Methodist Church, South, within the entire environs of his charge. Thus a holiness preacher, such as Morrison, could be prohibited from preaching in a camp meeting, tent meeting, or even within the church building of another denomination located in the vicinity of the objecting pastor's charge.

As a consequence of what he considered a new attempt to still the voice of men of his kind, Morrison temporarily withdrew from membership in the church during the late summer of 1898. The pastor of the Southern Methodist Church in Terrell, Texas, objected to Morrison's fulfilling his engagement to preach in a camp meeting to be held there in September. When Morrison had disregarded the protest of a pastor by preaching in Dublin two years earlier no law had been violated. To disregard the pastor's protest and go to Terrell as a Methodist minister would be ecclesiastically illegal. Since he had promised to be obedient to the discipline of the church so long as he continued in its connection, he avoided conflict by requesting his pastor to give him his church letter. As a member of no church he was subject to no ecclesiastical law while working in the Terrell camp meeting. He justified this peculiar action by saying:

> ...to go to Terrell over the protest of the pastor would be a plain violation of law. On the other hand to turn back from preaching to those starving souls at Terrell, who are pleading for the message of full salvation, would be to forfeit my self respect, to grieve the Holy Spirit, to discourage thousands of humble souls in whom by precept and example I have tried to

inspire that heroic Christian courage that would resist unto blood striving against sin.[8]

At heart Morrison was still a Southern Methodist. He made no plans to join any other church. Just when he returned to the church is unknown, but he was reinstated in plenty of time to be elected by his district conference as a lay delegate to the Annual Conference of 1901 and at that conference was elected as a lay delegate to the General Conference, which met in Dallas, Texas, the following spring. To make the situation still more ironic, Morrison not only returned to Texas, the scene of his great opposition, as a member of the General Conference, but friends pitched a big tent in Dallas and he preached to great throngs of people almost every night.

Before closing the Mountain Lake Park camp meeting in Maryland, in June 1904, Morrison once again was threatened with the use of ecclesiastical law as a means of discouraging his fervent presentation of the doctrine of entire sanctification. As in the former instances, the tension centered around a Texas meeting. Morrison received a letter from the Rev. R. H. Morris of Denton, Texas, in which he requested Morrison to cancel his engagement to preach in the Holiness Association camp meeting at Denton and that he not hold any other services within the bounds of the Denton station as long as Morris remained as pastor there. Morrison realized that to keep this engagement would now be a violation of the law. After carefully considering the whole problem he expressed his decision to his good friend, H. B. Cockrill.

> I have within me a conviction that I must go out and preach full salvation to the hungry multitudes; they have the law on me now, and I suppose they will enforce it and turn me out of the Church. That thought gives me a great pain, but I have something within me far more

valuable than church membership, and I shall be true to that conviction whatever comes.[9]

Morrison arrived in Denton on the evening of July 14, 1904. Only a day or two had gone by when he met the Reverend Mr. Morris, as he was driving in his buggy to notify Morrison that he must not preach in the community. Morrison went over to the buggy, shook hands with the preacher, and conversed for some minutes. This was indeed a serious occasion, but it was not too solemn for Morrison's Scotch-Irish nature to find something amusing.

> While I was talking with the brother and he was warning me that I must not preach, an immense red bedbug crawled out from some hiding place about his coat collar and walked deliberately up the lapel of his coat. It amused me so that my seriousness fled and it was with great difficulty that I restrained myself from bursting into laughter. While he was talking I was saying in my heart, "No man with bedbugs on him can run me out of a holiness camp meeting." It was the first, and only time, in a long and varied history and experience that one of these little creatures ever brought me any sort of comfort.[10]

The next day the minister came to the camp-ground to visit Morrison again and assure him that his second warning, in the presence of the old man who accompanied him, was in harmony with the *Discipline*, and that the next step would be to call his Church Board together to arrange for his trial. Morrison was deeply affected: "I broke down and cried, told him I loved my church, that I regretted to be turned out, and that the whole business was a deliberate purpose to stifle and hinder the preaching of the doctrine of Entire Sanctification as a second work of grace."[11] He then asked Morris to join him in prayer before he left. No sooner had the Rev. Mr. Morris concluded his prayer than Morrison "broke into a prayer, got happy, and praised the Lord."[12] According to Morrison, the old man who had accompanied his pastor as a witness began to weep, shook Morrison's hand warmly, and went with him to the tent where the service was being held. The pastor returned to the city alone and in disgust said that there was no use wasting time with that fellow Morrison and that he did not intend to bother with him any further. Nothing more was heard about a trial during the process of the camp meeting. This seemed to conclude the series of attempts to force Morrison either to leave the Methodist Episcopal Church, South, or to cease his preaching of holiness for his testimony was that this was "the last I have ever heard of any sort of protest or opposition to my holding camp meetings, conventions, or revivals throughout the Southland."[13]

Notes

[1] *The H. C. Morrison Case.*

[2] "The Daily Leader" (Lexington, Ky.).

[3] Conference Minutes (Kentucky Annual Conference of Methodist Episcopal Church, South). Hereafter referred to as "Conference Minutes."

[4] "Conference Minutes."

[5] *Ibid.*

[6] Arnold, *The H. C. Morrison Case, A State of Facts; An Investigation of the Law* (Louisville, 1897). Hereafter referred to as *The H. C. Morrison Case.*

[7] J. J. Tigert, ed., *The Doctrines and Discipline of the Methodist Episcopal Church, South.* Hereafter referred to as *The Doctrines and Discipline of the Methodist Episcopal Church.*

[8] *The Pentecostal Herald.*

[9] *Some Chapters of My Life Story.*

[10] *The Pentecostal Herald.*

[11] *Ibid.*

[12] *Ibid.*

[13] *The Pentecostal Herald.*

Chapter 7
First Presidency of Asbury College

It was during the summer of 1910, shortly after his return from a world tour of evangelism, that Henry Clay Morrison accepted the presidency of Asbury College. This began an association with educational institutions, which was to last for the thirty-two remaining years of his life. In order to obtain an appreciation of the responsibilities, which accompanied the administration of this college, it is necessary to review the history of the school.

Asbury College opened its doors as an educational institution on September 2, 1890, in Wilmore, Kentucky.[1] For some time the Rev. John Wesley Hughes, a minister in the Kentucky Conference of the Methodist Episcopal Church, South, had felt what he believed to be a call from God to start a school having as a major purpose the teaching of "full salvation." Upon the urgent invitation of the Methodist pastor, he came to Wilmore to investigate the possibilities offered by this village. When the businessmen of the community accepted his challenge to raise $1,600 for the proposed school within a period of one week, it was decided to locate the college here. Several acres of land were purchased and the construction of a four-room frame building was begun on July 13. From it's founding until the present time the doctrinal emphasis of this college has been upon a full and complete salvation for all men from all sin. This includes an emphasis upon the Wesleyan teaching of entire sanctification. So great has been this emphasis that the school was first named "Kentucky Holiness College." At that time there was probably not a single unorthodox school in Methodism, but though faithful to the fundamental doctrines "they neglected the Methodist doctrine of sanctification and put little emphasis on the study of the Bible."[2] It was for the purpose of emphasizing these that Hughes felt led to establish an interdenominational school. To insure the perpetuity of this objective the following statement was placed in the *Articles of Incorporations:*

> No president or teacher of said college shall ever be allowed to antagonize a full gospel. The Doctrines of Justification, Regeneration, Witness of the Spirit, and Entire Sanctification shall be sacred. It is chiefly to promote a true experience along these lines that the conduct of the institution was undertaken. This article shall never be altered or revoked. Should it ever cease to be in harmony with the above teachings or doctrines, the entire property belonging to or that may be acquired by this association shall revert to the National Association for the Promotion of Holiness to be carried on in harmony with their interpretation of entire sanctification.[3]

The name "Kentucky Holiness College," was satisfactory to neither its president, J. W. Hughes, nor to Bishop R. K. Hargrove. The former objected to it because it seemed to exclude many fundamental Christian doctrines to which he adhered; the latter objected on the ground that all Methodist schools were supposed to be holiness schools. Before the opening of school in the fall of 1891 the name was changed to "Asbury College" in honor of Bishop Francis Asbury. This seemed especially appropriate in view of the fact that Bishop Asbury has been largely responsible for the establishment of the first two Methodist schools in America. The second of these, Bethel Academy, founded in 1790, was located near High Bridge, Kentucky—about four miles from the present campus of Asbury College.

Hughes continued to operate Asbury College as a privately owned interdenominational college until early in 1904. Financial insecurity did not keep Hughes from carrying on an almost continual building program. In addition to the two buildings completed during the first year of the school's existence, four others were constructed: chapel and girl's dormitory in 1891, Minister's Hall in 1894, another girl's dormitory in 1899, and finally the large brick Administration Building in 1900. This latter was the crowning feature of the expansion program, containing not only class room and office space, but also a chapel with a seating capacity of nine hundred. The strain of carrying the responsibility for financing this program without outside assistance convinced Hughes that the school should be incorporated with a Board of Directors in control.

It was understood, at least by Hughes, that the change from individual to corporate ownership would not mean any change in its president. An appraisal committee evaluated the property at forty thousand dollars. Hughes agreed to accept twenty-five thousand as complete settlement. Fifteen thousand was to be paid in cash and the remainder was to be paid whenever convenient so long as Hughes still remained as president of the college. The ensuing year was filled with bitterness and intrigue, which finally resulted in radical changes in administration. Hughes resigned as president, though he remained on the teaching staff and Rev. Frank F. Fitch, of Marshall, Texas, was elected to the presidency.

The next five years constituted a period of instability for Asbury College. For some unexplained reason the Rev. Frank Fitch did not come to Wilmore, and during the month of July 1905, B. F. Haynes was elected as president of the college. The Board of Trustees leased the school to Haynes under terms, which made him completely responsible for all financial and administrative obligations. Having thus been released from the burden of collecting money for current expenses, the Board purchased the campus of Bellevue College, a Presbyterian school located on the north side of Wilmore. Haynes did not remain the full five-year term specified in his contract, but by mutual consent was released at the close of the school year 1907-1908. Since no immediate successor was obtained, Professor Newton Wray served as both dean and acting president throughout the following year. It was because a need was felt for the influence of a man more widely known than Dean Wray that someone else was sought as president. Dr. Aaron S. Watkins, a prominent leader in the prohibition movement, served the year 1909-1910, but he encountered opposition. As a result of rumors circulated during the year to the effect that his teaching was not thoroughly Wesleyan, it was agreed that his services should be terminated at the close of the school year in 1910.[4]

A disastrous fire the previous year had added to the financial instability of the college. On the morning of March 18, 1909, fire destroyed the Administration building and Music Hall of Asbury College. This loss of the two largest buildings on the campus caused a division among the members of the Board of Trustees as to the advisability of rebuilding on the same location. L. L. Pickett championed the cause of moving the school to some other part of the state, while H. C. Morrison, who was now a member of the board, favored keeping it in Wilmore. A most tempting offer came from John C. C. Mayo, who was connected with a small school in Paintsville, Kentucky. He offered the Asbury Board the campus of the school in Paintsville plus a cash gift of $50,000 if they would move Asbury College to that city. After careful consideration the board decided to retain the school in Wilmore providing the citizens would guarantee a gift of $15,000 toward the expense of rebuilding. Morrison carried the issue to the people of the community with such dramatic appeal that the total amount was soon subscribed. With this, another crisis passed and Asbury College continued to operate in Wilmore.

In rebuilding, the ten-acre Bellevue site offered a number of advantages both in location and buildings; therefore it was decided to centralize the program there. The construction of what is the present Administration Building and of Wesley Hall, a dormitory for men, continued throughout the year 1909-1910. In the attempt to obtain money with which to complete this project the Board of Trustees sold the old campus to the Wilmore Real Estate Company for $5,000.

The summer of 1910 found the Board facing a building program without sufficient funds and with no apparent means of obtaining them. The uncertainty of Asbury's future caused many students to transfer to other schools with the result that the list of prospective students for the fall of 1910 was very small. Furthermore, the school was once again without a president. It was in one of the desperate sessions of the Board during the summer that the members reached a unanimous decision to sell Asbury College and use the money to pay its debts unless Henry Clay Morrison would accept the presidency.

Henry Morrison had returned only a few weeks earlier from his tour around the world. He took time for a brief visit with his family before commencing his schedule of summer camp meetings. It was while engaged in the Silver Heights Camp meeting in Indiana that the delegate from the Asbury Board, the Rev. A. P. Jones, confronted him with their dilemma. The appeal to accept the presidency of the college was not easy to turn down, but its acceptance likewise presented problems. Morrison was not a trained educator. His professional life consisted of twenty-one years as editor and publisher of a religious paper, and thirty-one years as either a pastor or an evangelist. The opportunities in the field of evangelism had never seemed brighter. To venture into the field of college administration seemed hazardous. On the other hand he had known and supported Asbury College from its opening day, and the thought of closing her doors if he failed to respond to the challenge convinced him that he should accept. As a consequence, Morrison in less than two months after his return to America shifted from the role of fulltime evangelist to that of college president.

The situation at Asbury College when Henry Morrison assumed the office of president in the late summer of 1910 was disheartening to say the least. The ten-acre campus could boast of only four buildings. Two of these, the Administration Building and Wesley Hall, were still in the final stages of construction. Entrance to the Administration Building was through a side door, the main entrance not having been completed. There was no heating system other than the kerosene heaters carried from room to room by the professors, and the water supply consisted of shallow wells and three cisterns. The treasury was empty. Many of the faculty members had accepted other employment, and student body prospects were poor. In the opening chapel service there were only about fifty college students present. The one encouraging feature was that conditions could not get much worse.

In one of the first meetings of the Board of Trustees after Morrison became president he presented four administrative objectives: to secure an efficient faculty; to erect attractive buildings, and to improve the campus generally in order to provide an appealing and cultural atmosphere for study; to build the female department of the college in such a way as to attract young ladies who would have enough money to pay cash for their education; and to enlarge the teacher training program to enable the college to train teachers as well as preachers.[5] Underlying all of this was the imperative of obtaining sufficient financial support to meet current expenses.

Whatever else may be said regarding Morrison's qualifications as a college administrator, two factors can be listed in the column of assets. His extensive experience as an evangelist furnished many contacts from which both money and students might be solicited. Now as never before Morrison saw the advantage, which had come through the closing of doors of evangelistic opportunity in his own Kentucky Conference, thus forcing him to extend his labors across the nation and around the world. Students came to Asbury College as a result of these extensive contacts until finally it became known as the second most national college in America.[6] The other great asset to Morrison's administration was his paper, *The Pentecostal Herald*. The appeals to its 30,000 subscribers, affectionately called "The Herald Family," supplied a major source of the financial income for the college during the next three decades.

Aside from the many special appeals for money, two requests became traditional. Beginning in the fall of 1911 an appeal for a Thanksgiving offering became an annual call. The other drive was the Commencement offering. The large crowds attending the "Holiness Convention" at the conclusion of the academic year provided opportunity for taking a public offering. At times the total received in cash and pledges would reach $20,000.

Personal sacrifice on the part of Morrison played its part in keeping the school operating during the second decade of the twentieth century. For at least the first seven years of his administration he served without salary. Furthermore, much of his own money was given to the school for the purpose of buying equipment, paying operating expenses and professors' salaries. Morrison never entirely gave up his evangelistic work. This was especially true of his summer camp meeting schedule. When he received pay for his revivals or camp meetings he kept what was necessary for the support of his family and sent the remainder to help pay the teachers. "I would receive enough," Morrison said, "during my summer camp meetings to finish the back pay on their salaries. In this way I gave a good many thousands of dollars of which I kept no account."[7] When the school finally began paying its president a salary it was a modest $1,500. As late as 1922-1924 his salary was only $166.66 per month, plus room and board for three persons. During this period at least six of the professors were receiving higher salaries than that paid to the president.[8]

Morrison's sacrifice was not the only example of its kind, for, as he later testified, part of his willingness to do so grew out of the willingness of others to forego much for the sake of the college.

> …Automobiles came along, Wilmore filled up with them, but we stuck to old "Jim" and the surrey. A friend said to me, "Aren't you ashamed to drive around here in that old trap?" "Not in the least," was my reply. Thousands of one-dollar bills were coming to me from poor

people accompanied by a prayer, and the humble holiness people of the United States were building a great college at Wilmore, Ky.⁹

A business venture, which proved profitable for the college, was the purchase of a farm on January 15, 1916, at a cost of $35,000. The original purpose was to raise a large portion of the supplies needed in the dining hall, thereby reducing expenses in that department, and also to furnish employment for needy students. The program operated very well until the inflationary prices of land, caused by the United States' entrance into World War I made it seem advisable to sell the farm. The seventy thousand dollars received from its sale was used for the payment of some debts and the building of Fletcher Hall, a men's dormitory, and a college laundry. Morrison thought the income from the new dormitory would be greater than that realized from the farm, and the new laundry would furnish more student employment than the previous enterprise.

The fifteen years from 1910 to 1925 brought many changes in the physical plant of Asbury College. As has already been noted the campus comprised only four buildings when Morrison accepted the presidency; and two of them, Wesley Hall and the administration building were still under construction. Aside from their completion, the most pressing problem was a heating plant. Before the winter of 1910-1911 was over—but not before snow had fallen—a steam boiler was put into operation under a temporary shelter, and steam pipes were laid to the main buildings. In 1914 a new dining hall with a seating capacity of 175 was constructed. As the size of the college increased there was need of better equipment for the physical education department. As a result, work was begun during the summer of 1918 on the erection of a gymnasium and the building was completed during the following year. It was during the summer months of 1918 that Mary Crawford Hall, the largest of the girls' dormitories, was extensively enlarged and remodeled. Ample attractive dormitory facilities for women—one of Morrison's objectives for the building of the school—were thus provided. By 1919 there was need for a new and larger dining hall. Progress on its building was made during the summer but not rapidly enough to make the new hall usable at the opening of school that fall. Meals were prepared and eaten under the shelter of a tent until November 15 when the first meal was served in the new building. It was not until early in the spring of 1920, however, that the new dining hall was completed. Simultaneous with the construction of the dining hall was the erection of the new men's dormitory, Fletcher Hall, which was financed through the sale of the farm.

The years 1920 to 1922 brought three more changes to the campus. The first of these was the remodeling of the old Bellevue building to make it the equal of Mary Crawford Hall. It was renamed Glide Hall in honor of Mrs. Elizabeth Glide of San Francisco through whose generous gift the improvements had been made possible. In 1922 a brick building replaced the less permanent structure housing the heating plant. Extensive improvements were also made in the heating system itself. A climactic event of the year was the presentation by the graduating class of 1922 of an astronomical observatory housing a $1,000 telescope.

The building of Morrison Hall, or as it was frequently called, "The Theological Building," is worthy of special notice for it was not merely the addition of another building on the campus, but was in a sense the founding of Asbury Theological Seminary. Though the detailed account of the founding of this Seminary is related later it should be remembered that from its origin, Asbury College had stressed Bible study and related courses in theology. As the years of Morrison's administration continued, an increasing emphasis was placed upon ministerial training so that by 1922 about two hundred young people were in Asbury College preparing for the ministry. This interest in ministerial training stimulated Morrison to begin raising funds for a "Theological Building." In March 1922, Mrs. Glide of San Francisco pledged $20,000, providing an additional $30,000 is raised from other sources. Before the groundbreaking ceremony on June 1, 1922, $35,000 had been raised in cash and pledges. The three-story brick building, which was then, constructed furnished chapel, classrooms, and dormitory space for the Theological Department. Though the cornerstone bears the date, 1923, it was not formally dedicated until commencement 1925.

On April 21, 1924, fire once again brought disaster to the campus. The two main girls' dormitories, Glide Hall and Mary Crawford Hall, were completely destroyed. Fortunately, no one was injured, there was very little loss of personal property, and the buildings destroyed were covered by $128,000 insurance. At the time of the fire Morrison was on the train returning from a meeting in Amarillo, Texas. Officials at the college were not able to contact him so he first heard the news from a Methodist minister who boarded the train the next day. For some time Morrison had been suffering from heart trouble and his friends were concerned lest this shocking news might be too great a strain for him. When, to their surprise, he arrived on the campus with no apparent results of shock they asked how the news of the fire had affected him. "A man on the train broke the news to me," Morrison said, "but God had so blessed me in my devotions on the train that morning, that I was prepared for the news of the fire. It had no more effect upon me than a gnat lighting on the trunk of an elephant in South Africa."[10]

The practical approach to the loss of the two girls' dormitories is seen by the dispatch with which plans for a new building were formulated. During the two days intervening between his arrival on the campus and his departure for Detroit, Michigan, necessary equipment was purchased and the boys of the college were organized into groups for the purpose of clearing away the debris of the fire. By May 14, 1924, architects had drawn plans for a new building; a contractor had been engaged, and excavation preparatory to construction had begun. Work on the building progressed rapidly and rooms were made available to the girls soon after the opening of school that fall. Glide-Crawford Hall, a three-story brick building, was dedicated during the week of Commencement in May 1925.

Students as well as material equipment are necessary, however, to the advancement of a college; and an examination of the records indicates that the increase in enrollment was commensurate with the improvements in educational facilities. The total registration for Morrison's first year, 1910-1911, was 212. The first commencement saw only four graduates. At the end of the first five years the student roll showed a total of 356, twenty-one of who were granted degrees that year. The largest enrollment for the fifteen-year period, 1910-1925, was the year 1924-1925 when 556 young people were in attendance. The largest graduating class thus far in the history of the school was in 1925, the year Morrison resigned, when degrees were conferred upon ninety-two young men and women.

Besides widespread representation from the various sections of the United States, students from several foreign countries were in attendance. The increased number of students coming from such widespread geographic areas has been credited largely to the personal influence of Morrison and to *The Pentecostal Herald*. His intense missionary zeal not only attracted foreign students to attend Asbury College, but also encouraged its graduates to choose foreign missionary work as their vocation. In 1922, sixty-six graduates were presenting the message of Christianity in foreign lands. The following year a newspaper reporter made the statement that "Asbury furnishes more foreign missionaries than any other school in America, irrespective of size, which is a remarkable record."[11] By 1929, the number had grown to more than one hundred. Outstanding among this group were Bishop Fred B. Fisher and E. Stanley Jones, Missionaries to India.

Morrison was just as influential in student life and government on the campus as he was in persuading students to attend Asbury College. "He was the dominating influence," said one alumnus. "He furnished the inspiration for the program, set its bounds and required it to revolve in the orbit he fixed."[12] Another said, "He was a benevolent despot, who loved and fathered his institutions, but perhaps erred in dominating them too much."[13] His influence was "dominant in the life of every student! He loved them, corrected them, and backed them financially."[14] Whenever Dr. Morrison returned to the campus there seemed to be a difference... He was fatherly, interested in the students and all that concerned them."[15] As Morrison would walk across the campus his long white hair and his Prince Albert coat gave him the appearance of a prophet preacher from another generation. The stern set of his jaw indicated that he would tolerate no violations of the rules of the school, but the mischievous twinkle in his eye and his sense of humor revealed the more human side of his nature. Only a few people have the ability possessed by Morrison to be stern and unrelenting, and yet tenderhearted and forgiving in spirit.

The concern of the administration for the spiritual and moral welfare of the students is demonstrated by rules and customs of the college. A fall revival, usually held shortly after registration, was one of the first efforts to reach the unconverted among the student body. Throughout the year regular attendance at the chapel services and the Friday evening meeting of the Holiness Band was compulsory. Such social evils as the use of tobacco, or intoxicating liquors and participation in other types of "wordy amusement" were strictly prohibited. As late as 1918-1919, the girls were required on all public occasions to wear dark blue uniforms and black mortarboard caps. Even after uniformity of dress was no longer required "there were days when Dr. Morrison like a father admonished young women in Asbury College not to testify if their breast pin hung too low, and when he sent them back to their rooms to redress if skirts were suggestive of the worldliness of the day."[16]

In 1910 the academic standards of Asbury College were low. Obtaining an efficient faculty and raising the educational value of its work sufficiently to receive accreditation by the state were among the early objectives presented to the Board of Trustees by Morrison. Throughout the first year of his leadership Asbury had a faculty of seventeen members, only one of who had a Master's degree. Eight of the seventeen did not have any earned degrees.[17] At the beginning of Morrison's second term as president, he having been re-elected in December 1914, for another five-year period, two professors boasted Master of Arts degrees, and one theology teacher was a graduate of a theological seminary having earned the Bachelor of Divinity degree. The *Catalogue of Asbury College* still listed five faculty members as not having any earned degrees.

Through the years there was gradual improvement in the scholastic qualifications of the faculty until in 1924-1925 the teaching staff of the College of Arts and Sciences included one member holding a Doctor of Philosophy degree from Columbia University, one with a Doctor of Medicine degree, and six

Master of Arts. Only one professor, G. W. Ridout, possessed no earned degree, but he was in the department of practical theology, where actual experience in the field was a valuable background for teaching.

Asbury, as did so many small-unaccredited colleges in the period embracing the turn of the century, conferred Masters as well as Bachelors degrees. From 1895 to 1912, nineteen persons received the degree of Master of Arts from Asbury College. It is to Morrison's credit that only one of these was given during his administration. The emphasis was shifted to the conferring of the honorary degree of Doctor of Divinity upon worthy candidates. The first of these was given to Fred B. Fisher in 1915. One of the most noted men to be given this honor, however, was E. Stanley Jones.

Without doubt the greatest academic achievement of Morrison's first administration was the accreditation, which Asbury College received in 1921. At this time it was given recognition by the University of Kentucky as a standard grade A college. At the same time it was certified by the state of Kentucky for teacher training, thus reaching another of Morrison's objectives. The College had now obtained the highest credit rating given by the state. Any further advance in this direction could be obtained only from regional associations.

The years of Morrison's presidency were fraught with problems common to such an office. Some of them were made more difficult, however, because of his own personality and his method of attacking problems. He possessed a lordly personality, which at times made it difficult for him to cooperate with his colleagues. This masterful type of leadership served a purpose in holding the institution together during very trying days, but it was hard to maintain during those long periods when the reins of control were held only loosely by

Morrison because he was away from the campus conducting revival meetings. During his absence authority necessarily devolved upon other administrative officers. At times Morrison seemed to suspect those who necessarily assumed this responsibility as being rivals for his office. This may account in part for their having been at least four vice-presidents—and four years in which this office was not filled—during the fifteen years of Morrison's control. His frequent and often extended absences from the campus at times left him with inadequate information upon which to base administrative decisions. Inequities, which resulted sometimes, increased the problems rather than contributing to their solution.

The suffering caused by a weakened heart had convinced Morrison that he must relinquish some of his responsibilities. Since early in 1923 he had been seeking a man with qualifications to carry on the leadership of Asbury College. It was not until the year 1924-1925 that he found such a man in Dr. Lewis Robeson Akers who was that year serving as vice-president. At the meeting of the Board of Trustees on June 1, 1925, Morrison stated that his term of office expired at that meeting and that he would not be a candidate for reelection. He then nominated Dr. L. R. Akers, who was elected by a unanimous vote. The fact that Morrison's refusal to accept re-election was voluntary, and not because of opposition on the part of the Board, can be seen by noting that he was immediately unanimously elected as President of Asbury Theological Seminary, Vice-President of Asbury College, and President of the Board of Trustees.[18]

Two days later Morrison presented diplomas to more than one hundred members of the graduating class. Following this he made a public statement of his resignation and commended his successor, Dr. Akers, to the confidence of the people. In his Diary he expressed his sense of relief as he closed fifteen years as executive leader of Asbury College: "Thank God for the release of this responsibility. May His blessing rest upon my successor."[19]

Notes

[1] John Wesley Hughes, *The Autobiography of John Wesley Hughes, D.D.* (Louisville, 1923). Digital copy freely available from First Fruits Press:
<http://place.asburyseminary.edu/firstfruitsheritagematerial/18/>

[2] *The Pentecostal Herald.*

[3] "Articles of Incorporation of Asbury College."

[4] Earl Stanley McKee, "The Early History of Asbury College, 1890-1910" (Unpublished M.A. thesis, University of Kentucky, 1926). Hereafter referred to as "The Early History of Asbury College."

[5] *The Pentecostal Herald.*

[6] New York *Times.*

[7] *Some Chapters of My Life Story.*

[8] "Faculty Meeting Minutes of Faculty of Asbury College."

[9] *The Pentecostal Herald.*

[10] H. C. Morrison, "Diary," 1893, 1895-1910; 1913-41.

[11] *The Pentecostal Herald.*

[12] "Asbury Alumni Questionnaire." A questionnaire mailed to 200 alumni of Asbury College and Asbury Theological Seminary. Hereafter referred to as "Asbury Alumni Questionnaire."

[13] *Ibid.*

[14] *Ibid.*

[15] "Faculty Meeting Minutes of Faculty of Asbury College."

[16] "Asbury Alumni Questionnaire."

[17] *Catalogue of Asbury College.*

[18] "Minutes of the Annual Meeting of the Board of Trustees of Asbury College."

[19] H. C. Morrison, "Diary," 1893, 1895-1910; 1913-41.

Chapter 8
Expanding Influence

The pressing demands placed upon Henry Morrison as President of Asbury College did not keep him away from the evangelistic work, which he loved so much. Actually it was the remuneration received from this activity, which not only furnished the necessary support for his family during the first seven years of his presidency of the college, but also aided greatly in balancing the budget of the school. Although his services varied somewhat from that of the two previous decades, his influence was perhaps never greater than during the years 1910-1925.

The best source of information relative to Morrison's evangelistic activity during this period- his personal diaries- is incomplete. During the first two or three years of his executive leadership of the college, it seems he was too busy to make daily entries in his journal. In spite of these omissions, however, there is record of his participation in more than two hundred and sixty revival meetings or conventions during the fifteen-year period under consideration. The average was only slightly under the twenty per year maintained prior to his election as President of Asbury College. These engagements took him into thirty-five states, Canada, England, and Continental Europe. He entered three states in which he had not previously conducted services-Florida, North Carolina, and Washington.[1]

Morrison continued to hold protracted meetings of two and three weeks' duration in which many souls were saved, but there was a marked increase in the number of invitations to speak to holiness conventions, Bible conferences, and preachers' meetings, many of which continued for only one week or even less.[2] At least two reasons may be given for this shift of emphasis. The demands of the college made long absences from the campus unadvisable. Perhaps more important, however, was the probability that his position as an experienced evangelist and also the prestige associated with being a college president created a demand for his services as one qualified to instruct groups of Christian workers. An example of this type of ministry may be seen through the invitations received by Morrison to be one of the lecturers in four of the Summer Schools for Preachers conducted by the Methodist Church, South, in the summer of 1921.[3]

Camp meeting preaching was not neglected. Even the incomplete data available lists fifty-eight camp meetings in which Morrison was engaged during the years 1911-1925. According to his own account as written in 1927, he had been a camp meeting preacher for thirty-five years. "This," he said, "would figure out something more than eight solid years on camp meeting grounds or enroute going and coming from camps." He estimated that he had preached "at least 2,500 times at camp meetings." At times as many as fifty seekers came forward after a single sermon, and frequently there were five to ten.[4] The invitations he received to be one of the speakers in the famous camp meeting at Ocean Grove, New Jersey, constituted one of the noteworthy aspects of his ministry. Here the tabernacle was said to seat 10,000 people, and it was usually well filled for all services.[5]

As the years went by, Morrison became more closely associated with the Methodist Episcopal Church, South, and his influence in it became increasingly greater. The Kentucky Annual Conference re-admitted him to membership in 1911, and at the request of the Conference, he was appointed by Bishop Warren A. Candler as President of Asbury College.[6] He continued to receive a similar appointment each year so long as he served in that capacity.

Not only was Morrison re-admitted into the Conference, but also the Bishops began to request that he be the special speaker during the sessions. During the fall of 1920 he preached to nine Annual Conferences. Bishop U. V. W. Darlington invited him to four such meetings in North and South Carolina. The following year he had invitations to preach at fourteen Annual Conferences,[7] but previous engagements and other conflicts prevented him from accepting half of these. During the years 1913-1924 Morrison was special speaker at thirty Annual Conferences in the Southern Methodist Church and addressed five Conferences of other denominations. On at least five different occasions he was asked to preside over his own Kentucky Conference while the Bishop was engaged in other business.[8] What a far cry this was from his situation a few years earlier when he had been expelled from the church and its ministry on a charge of insubordination!

During this general period Morrison was also elected as a delegate and served in four General Conferences of the Methodist Episcopal Church, South. In 1917 he was first elected as a clerical delegate to the General Conference.[9] Arrangements were made for Morrison and Bishop John C. Kilgo to alternate in conducting evangelistic services each evening during this Methodist gathering in Atlanta. U. V. W. Darlington was ordained a Bishop at this time, and Morrison was credited as having an influential part in his election. In recognition of his influence and friendship, Morrison was asked to be the principal speaker at a banquet given on May 16, 1918, in honor of the new Bishop.[10]

Four years later Morrison was again elected delegate to the General Conference which met in Hot Springs, Arkansas, May 3-19, 1922. During this session he was placed on the Committee on Doctrine, one of the important divisions of the organization. Some earnest debates followed as a result of the conflict between conservative and liberal theologians within the group.[11] Before the close of the Conference some of Morrison's friends expressed a desire to put his name up for election as Bishop. Although there seemed fair prospects for the success of such an effort, Morrison definitely refused to consider any such move.[12]

By virtue of being a delegate in 1922 he became a member of the Special Conference called to meet in Chattanooga, Tennessee, in July 1924, to consider the question of union between the two great branches of American Methodism. Morrison was chairman of the Kentucky delegation to the General Conference, which met in Memphis, Tennessee in 1926, and was appointed to two regular Conference Committees—Episcopal, and Education and Publication. He also served on a special sub-committee created to investigate charges placed against Bishop W. F. McMurry relative to some financial transactions made while conducting church business. According to Morrison's memoranda, he also took an active part in the debates on the floor of the Conference.

In addition to having been several times elected as a delegate to the General Conference, Morrison had the distinction of being appointed by the Bishops as a delegate to the Ecumenical Conference of Methodism meeting in London, September 6-16, 1921. This was considered to be one of the highest honors bestowed by the church, other than the election to the bishopric. Morrison left New York City on July 23; and after spending several weeks traveling in England, France, Belgium, Germany, and Holland, he arrived in London in time to participate in the worldwide meeting of Methodism. Upon his return to the United States his schedule was filled until December by invitations to speak before Annual Conferences in Texas, Oklahoma, and Mississippi.[13]

Many changes came in Morrison's personal and family life during those years when he was busy as college executive, lecturer, evangelist, and church leader. Six and a half years after settling in Wilmore, death and sorrow once again came to his home. While still living in their home at O'Bannon, Mrs. Morrison had injured her leg in a fall, and an infection of the bone made amputation necessary.[14] It should not be implied, however, that the wearing of an artificial leg, or declining health adversely affected an otherwise sparkling personality. She not only "managed well her own household," but after moving to Wilmore also taught Bible courses in the college and gave many hours to counseling with students. Those who knew her during those last years of her life speak of her as having a radiant personality and being one of the most devout Christians they had ever known. Her health failed rapidly during the year 1913, and by January of the following year the doctors gave little hope for substantial improvement. She died in their home in Wilmore on the afternoon of March 23, 1914. Funeral services were held on March 25, and interment was made in the Wilmore cemetery.

The Morrison family was broken up and the children separated after the death of their mother. The oldest daughter, Geneva, was sent to Logan Female College at Russellville, Kentucky, for three years (1914-1917) where she took pre-college courses. The oldest son, Howard, attended Asbury College until 1917, when he enlisted in the army. He, along with his two half-brothers, Bain and Henry, were in active duty in France during World War 1. Howard suffered injuries there, which were factors in causing his death in 1929. The three younger children, Franklin, Emily, and Helen, were cared for by their Aunt Emma. They returned to the family home in O'Bannon where they lived until 1916. Sometime during the latter half of that year they returned to Wilmore where Mrs. Emma Pritchard continued to make a home for them. Somewhat more than a year later Helen went to live with her half-sister, Mrs. Laura Young, while Franklin and Emily remained as students at Asbury College. In June 1920 the Morrisons moved once more- this time to Louisville.[15]

"Dr. Morrison, with all of his world interests, and the great demands on his time, still tried to be a good father," wrote Ralph A. Curtis, "and I felt he succeeded in doing so."[16] Although away from his family a major portion of the time, he never seemed to enjoy that separation. A diary entry in 1916 revealed his attitude. "Helen is my baby girl, six years of age. So dear to my heart. We have lived apart so much of our lives. She is inexpressibly dear to me. My Lord save and bless her." A year later he wrote: "My heart longs inexpressibly to be with my little children. They need a Father so badly. Oh my God, take care of them for me and thee."[17] One would expect that as a minister he would be deeply concerned over the spiritual welfare of his family, and so he was. "I have much for which to praise God. My daughter Annie Laura has been beautifully sanctified. Howard and Franklin my sons have been converted...[18]

On Thursday evening, February 17, 1916, H. C. Morrison and Mrs. Bettie Whitehead were married at her home in Louisville by the Rev. S. H. Lovelace. Bettie Whitehead Morrison was born in 1866, the daughter of Augustus and Amanda Leichardt. Her first husband was Dr. G. W. Whitehead, a promising physician. Upon his early death she was left with one son, George Garland. For a number of years Mrs. Whitehead taught music at Asbury College and later at Taylor University. In 1906 she had joined the staff of *The Pentecostal Herald* and had been associated with Morrison in his work since that date.

H. C. Morrison and "Aunt Bettie," as she came to be known, worked together throughout the remainder of his life as an efficient team. She frequently traveled with him in his evangelistic work where her talents as a musician aided greatly in the services. Her ability to do secretarial work enabled him to dictate many of his letters and his editorials for *The Herald*. When she was not traveling with him she worked as a capable assistant editor in the office of *The Herald*. "There is no possible doubt," wrote his daughter Geneva, "that she (Aunt Bettie) added years to his life and multiplied his service."[19]

A more personal picture of Dr. Morrison may be portrayed through some incidents, which are recorded in his writings for the years closely associated with his sixtieth birthday.[20] By that time his hair, which he wore in long flowing locks, was white. This, combined with the Prince Albert coat, which was usually a part of his attire, gave him a dignified, almost "prophetic" appearance. His firm set jaw indicated a stern personality, but the twinkle of his eye let one know that he was willing to be a friend. Neither his firm stride nor his manner of living indicated his age or the physical infirmities, which were slowly but surely weakening him. At sixty, he still rose between four and five in the morning in order to enjoy some time in the family garden before starting his scheduled work of the day. On many days his diary records his traveling the eighty miles from Wilmore to Louisville, and arriving at the offices of the Pentecostal Publishing Company by 8:30 or 9:00 in the morning. A diary entry for February 2, 1915, gave an example of an ordinarily busy day. After leading the chapel service he dictated a number of letters and then met with a delegation of students anxious to go out and preach. Following a faculty meeting he conferred with a Mr. Lowery about cosigning a note for $5,000 with the college. He met with an executive committee of the College board, signed 120 letters, and concluded the day by finishing work on a lecture on prophecy.[21] Morrison never regained the physical strength of former years after having suffered with amoebic dysentery, contracted on his evangelistic tour of the Orient in 1909-1910. After his having received treatment for this condition, available records do not indicate the development of any other major physical weakness prior to 1917 when he collapsed in his office after having given a talk in the college chapel. The doctors suggested the cause as being a "nervous break." From that time there are numerous indications in Morrison's diary that there was increasing physical weakness. While holding a revival in Columbus, Ohio, in April 1920, he noticed that his heart was skipping beats. A physical examination disclosed that he was suffering from leakage of the heart and also that the heart was enlarged to nearly twice its normal size. This so frightened Morrison that he decided to discontinue the preaching of three sermons per day. Later in the summer of that same year he felt the effect of high altitudes upon his weakened heart when he over-taxed his strength and fainted while preaching in the camp meeting at Mountain Lake Park, Maryland. For the remainder of his life Morrison realized that his activities must be governed by the ability of his heart to stand the strain to which it would be subjected.[22] Something of the story of those years will be told in a later chapter.

Notes

[1] *A Biographical Sketch of Henry Clay Morrison.*

[2] *Remarkable Conversions.*

[3] H. C. Morrison, "Diary," 1893, 1895-1910; 1913-41.

[4] "Articles of Incorporation, The Morrison Theological Trust" (Louisville, Sept. 18, 1942).

[5] "The Revival of the Camp Meeting by the Holiness Groups."

[6] Letter from H. C. Morrison written to John Paul from Shanghai, China, March 16, 1910.

[7] *The Pentecostal Herald.*

[8] H. C. Morrison, "Diary," 1893, 1895-1910; 1913-41.

[9] "Conference Minutes."

[10] "The Early History of Asbury College."

[11] New York *Times.*

[12] "Faculty Meeting Minutes of Faculty of Asbury College."

[13] Letter to the author from E. B. Vargas, Jan. 25, 1954.

[14] Letter to the author from Mrs. Geneva Morrison Mendenhall, March 31, 1954. Hereafter referred to as "Letter from Mrs. Geneva Morrison Mendenhall."

[15] H. C. Morrison, "Diary," 1893, 1895-1910; 1913-41.

[16] "Asbury Alumni Questionnaire."

[17] H. C. Morrison, "Diary," 1893, 1895-1910; 1913-41.

[18] *Ibid.*

[19] "Letter from Mrs. Geneva Morrison Mendenhall."

[20] Ohio Northern University granted to Morrison the honorary D.D. degree in 1909.

[21] H. C. Morrison, "Diary," 1893, 1895-1910; 1913-41.

[22] As a result of his heart condition, Morrison finally consented to the purchase of his first automobile, a Dodge, during the summer of 1923.

Chapter 9
Second Presidency of Asbury College

When H. C. Morrison resigned from the presidency of Asbury College in June 1925, he nominated Dr. Lewis R. Akers as his successor. He was unanimously elected as president for a term of one year. Since Akers did not have an outside source of income, as had Morrison, the board voted an annual salary of $4,000 plus free house rent and some other allowances for educational expenses. The salary was later raised to $5,000 and then to $6,000 per year. These actions may have been somewhat indicative of the financial difficulties, which were to accompany the Akers' administration through the years 1925-1932.

Credit should be given to Dr. Akers for the progress, which was made during the years of his leadership. The student enrollment continued to increase until it reached a peak of 639 for the year 1928-29, and maintained an average of 582 for the eight-year period.[1]

A very acceptable corollary to the enlarged student body was the continual improvement in the educational qualifications of the faculty. During the last year of his administration only four faculty members did not have graduate degrees and the number holding the doctorate had increased from one in 1925 to six in 1933. The higher scholastic rating thus achieved brought to the school corresponding recognition among educational associations.

The building program, which had been started in 1918, continued for some time. During the closing years of Morrison's first administration a campaign had been started to raise funds for the erection of a new library building. The groundbreaking ceremony was conducted by Drs. Morrison and Akers on May 30, 1925. The following year the construction was completed and the library was moved into its new building. Probably the outstanding achievement under Dr. Akers' leadership was the building of Hughes' Memorial Auditorium in 1928-1929.

This expansion was very expensive, and since few people expected the prosperity of the late 1920's to end in the financial crash of 1929, the school faced the depression years of the early thirties with a total indebtedness of nearly $600,000. As a gesture indicating his concern over the situation, Dr. Akers offered to contribute fifteen percent of his salary for the year 1931-1932. The following year he increased this to twenty percent, and a majority of the faculty donated ten percent of their salaries. The continued strain of this financial situation proved too much for Dr. Akers. As early as September 4, 1933, he told Dr. Morrison that his health was breaking and that he would not be able to continue as President of Asbury College. On September 19, 1933, while a patient in The Christ Hospital in Cincinnati, Ohio, he wrote the Executive Committee of Asbury College tendering his resignation and recommending that Morrison be asked to serve as acting president until a successor could be chosen.

In accord with the suggestion made by Dr. Akers, the Executive Committee agreed unanimously to ask Morrison to serve as acting president. Although Morrison was then seventy-six years of age and had been in poor health for some time, he accepted the challenge. In many respects the situation paralleled that of 1910. In June 1933, the business manager reported that the total indebtedness was approaching the half million mark. It was little wonder that many felt the school was likely to close its doors any day.

Upon resuming the presidency of the college Morrison felt that one way to balance the budget would be through administrative economies. Earl Savage, a well-to-do Lexington business man, who had just assumed the duties of business manager, was serving without salary, and for two years Morrison did likewise. According to Morrison's estimate the consequent saving in administrative expense amounted to nearly $15,000 per year. With this example of self-sacrifice on their part they felt free to ask others to make gifts to the school.

The financial problem received the major attention of the administration during the year 1933-34. One of the first projects was to get together enough money to save the homes of the professors. Because salaries had not been paid in full, faculty members had been unable to meet their payments to building and loan associations. With the aid of H. H. McAfee as field agent, $20,000 in donations were received to meet this emergency. During the fall months the President and the Business Manager met with and presented the school's financial picture to many of its creditors with the result that many made donations to the college, few pressed for payment and thus sufficient time was given to collect money and eventually to make satisfactory settlement of all accounts.

In June 1934, the faculty signed a petition and presented it to the Board of Trustees asking that if possible Dr. Morrison be retained as president for another year. At the annual meeting of that board, on June 4, he was unanimously elected for a term of one year. Because of his age, the term of office was not extended for a longer period, but he was reelected each year through 1940.

Morrison spent the winter months of each year in the South because of his age and health; so it was deemed advisable to elect a vice-president who would have executive authority in the absence of the president. Upon his recommendation, the Executive Committee of the Board of trustees appointed Dr. Z. T. Johnson to this office for a term beginning March 1 and extending to September 1, 1935, with the understanding that on the approval of the Board of Trustees he should be elected for a term of one year, beginning on the latter date. Dr. Johnson was an alumnus of Asbury College, having received his Bachelor of Arts degree in 1925. Four years later he received the Doctor of Philosophy degree from George Peabody College for Teachers. At the time of his election he was pastor of the Methodist Episcopal Church, South, in Wilmore, Kentucky.

With the inclusion of Johnson as a member of the executive staff of Asbury College the drive toward payment of the debt made steady progress. According to a report given in June 1935, by Earl Savage, business manager, the indebtedness had been reduced by more than $190,000, though the balance still remained at slightly over a quarter million dollars. Following the resignation of Mr. Savage on September 9, the Board of Trustees authorized Z. T. Johnson to serve as both Business Manager and Vice-President of the college. The team of Morrison and Johnson now went to work in earnest to payoff the balance of the debt. By March 1937 the debt had been reduced to $90,300 and a complete wiping out of this obligation was set as their goal.[2] Accompanying the debt clearance campaign, efforts were also being made to increase endowment funds for the college. During year 1936-37, one large gift of

$137,000 was given by Mrs. Rebecca Talbott of Ohio. This was set aside as endowment money to be administrated by a special trust fund committee. As a means of immediate investment, $60,300 was loaned to the college in order to clear notes with outside business concerns. As a result, Asbury College was able to make full payment of all financial obligations to outside organizations and the canceled bonds were burned in a great victory service held on May 11, 1938.

Efforts to raise money continued, however, and on October 6 a check for $18,500 "completed payment in full of the $60,300 note given to the Talbott Endowment Committee...and also represents the full and final payment on the indebtedness of the college."[3] Credit for this achievement should be given to Morrison for his courage, faith, and vision; to the sacrificial giving of "The Herald Family," whose loyalty to Asbury College and the doctrines for which it stood had been cultivated for a period of forty years; and to Z. T. Johnson, who kept the school operating with a balanced budget and carefully managed the business interests of the college in its debt-clearance campaign.

Another major achievement of Morrison's second administration was the rapid growth of the endowment fund. When he resumed the duties of the president, these resources amounted to a little less than $130,000. At the time of Morrison's resignation in 1940, the figures were in excess of half a million. The largest single gift was that bequeathed by Mrs. Talbott in 1937. A part of this money was invested in the 320 acre Asbury-Talbott farm, which has been operated by the college ever since its purchase. Much of this land is that which was previously owned by the college and sold during the period of inflated prices in 1919. The price for which it was repurchased was considerably less than the amount received by the college from its sale a few years before. The balance of the

Talbott fund was used in the construction of a hotel building located in Wilmore. It was to be known as the Talbott Hotel. Upon its completion, however, it was rented to Asbury Theological Seminary and was utilized as an administration building.

Pecuniary interests did not absorb the entire attention of the administration, however. Student enrollment was maintained at an average of 556 per year—a decrease from that of the Akers' administration but one, which is understandable since these were years of economic depression. The standard of academic training among faculty members was maintained at the level achieved during the closing years of the former administration. The outstanding accomplishment in the scholastic realm, however, was the attaining, on April 12, 1940, of full membership in the Southern Association of Colleges and Secondary Schools—thus making Asbury College a fully accredited school.[4] A major portion of the credit for this belongs to Dr. Johnson, though he constantly had the moral support of Morrison in the efforts to meet the standards of membership set by the Southern Association.

Although the board continued year by year to elect him as President of the College the uncertainties of his leadership because of both age and impaired health were fully realized; therefore, in 1937 the board elected Dr. Johnson as Executive Vice-President for a four year term. It was further provided "that in any event of a vacancy in the office of the Presidency of Asbury College, he [Johnson] shall automatically become President of the College for the remaining portion of the unexpired term of his election."

Following his re-election in 1939 Morrison stated "he would accept, cheerfully serve for another year but that he would in no case and under no consideration accept the office of President any further." He went on to explain "he did not care to retain the honor when the actual burden of the operation of the college rested so heavily upon the shoulders of the Executive Vice-President."[5] This did not imply, however, that he felt Johnson should be made President. When, at the time of the meeting of the Board of Trustees in 1940, the order of business called for the election of president, Morrison nominated Dr. Paul Rees, a well-known evangelist. Dr. Johnson then nominated Morrison. Johnson was also nominated, but asked that his name be withdrawn. The ballots were cast for Rees and Morrison with the result that Morrison was elected by a vote of twenty to five. After his election Morrison immediately resigned. In harmony with the previous action of the Board in 1937, Dr. Z. T. Johnson automatically became President of the College for the remainder of his term, or until 1941. The Board then voted unanimously to give their support to Johnson as the chief executive of the school. Upon a motion made by Johnson, Morrison was then elected President Emeritus for life with an annual salary of $2,400.

Although Morrison retained a feeling of disappointment long after the closing of school in June 1940, his sincere concern for the welfare of Asbury College was doubtless expressed in the words of an editorial written for the *Pentecostal Herald*. "In retiring from the presidency of the school I feel the deepest interest in my successor. I believe and pray that he may be a better man for the place than I have been. He cannot love the institution any better than I have, and do, give to it more liberally than I have, stand more firmly for the great principles and Bible truth it emphasizes and promulgates than I have."[6] Morrison never ceased to be an ardent supporter of Asbury College.

Notes

[1] *Remarkable Conversions.*

[2] "Minutes of the Annual Meeting of the Board of Trustees of Asbury College."

[3] "Minutes of the Executive Committee of the Board of Trustees of Asbury College." Hereafter referred to as "Minutes of the Executive Committee."

[4] *Ibid.*

[5] "Minutes of the Annual Meeting of the Board of Trustees of Asbury College."

[6] *The Pentecostal Herald.*

Chapter 10
Under the Cloud of Ill Health

The twelve years immediately following H. C. Morrison's first resignation in 1925, as President of Asbury College, constituted a period of evangelism frequently interrupted by intervals of severe illness. Retirement, however, did not mean abandonment of all public activity, for the records show that within less than four months he was engaged as a speaker in nine series of meetings, seven of which were camp meetings. These engagements took him into eight different states.

The ensuing year Morrison filled twenty-one different engagements, extending into fourteen states. Of these meetings nine were camp meetings, two were Annual Conferences, and one was the General Conference of the Methodist Episcopal Church, South, which met in Memphis, Tennessee.

As had been his custom for several years, he spent the winter months in the warm climate of Florida. This year he remained in Miami from January 4, until March 24, 1926. Morrison felt that the cottage they had built five years before was in too congested an area of the city and so he arranged for the building of another in a more quiet and restful suburban section of Miami. Aside from the personal convenience of this transaction, he thought that a cottage here would be a good investment, which could be left to his two unmarried daughters, Emily and Helen, in case he should not live long.

Soon after leaving Florida, Morrison sought a doctor's advice regarding an ailment, which was to plague him for the remainder of his life. After an X-ray examination this doctor pronounced the difficulty an ulcer, for which no permanent cure was ever effected. Many diary entries record instances of Morrison being unable to sleep because of the pain. Though causing much suffering, this new ailment seldom stopped him from continuing his work as an evangelist.

As a younger man Morrison had thought that should he live to be seventy years of age he would retire from active service and live in his little country home in O'Bannon, Kentucky. There he would cultivate a garden and care for a cow and some chickens. Such a life would give him plenty of time for relaxation, reading the Bible and other good books, and visiting with his friends. But when his seventieth birthday came he said: "...I find that preaching is delightful, the need is great, the people are hungering for the gospel, and there is no question in my mind with regard to my duty; so long as the Lord may give me strength I shall go on preaching."[1]

The activities of 1927 indicate that Morrison fulfilled what he considered to be his duty. While "resting" in Miami during the month of February he wrote a book, *The Optimism of Pre-Millennialism*[2]. During the remainder of the year his schedule comprised fourteen revival campaigns or conventions, seven camp meetings, and five Annual Conferences. In these he preached at least 312 times—an active life for a man in his seventy-first year.

An illustration of Morrison's evangelistic fervor may be seen through the work of The Evangelical Methodist League sponsored by him. It was in 1924 that he first proposed the idea of creating an organization composed of loyal members of the Methodist church who desired to see the Bible doctrines as held by John Wesley and the early Methodists not only preserved but proclaimed through evangelistic preaching. Those interested were to join the organization by sending their names and contributions to the office of the Pentecostal Publishing Company in Louisville. The money received was used in the purchase of tents, which were then utilized, by evangelists and evangelistic parties in conducting revival campaigns in places where such meetings would not likely be sponsored by anyone else. Many of the gospel teams were composed of energetic young student preachers from Asbury College. During the summer of 1928 about forty tents were being used. It was estimated that as a result of the program several thousand heard the Gospel preached and many were converted.

A distinct honor came to Morrison on June 6, 1928, when Asbury College conferred upon him the degree of Doctor of Laws. He was the recipient of the first such degree ever granted by that College. At first Morrison understood that it was to be given on the basis of scholarship and refused to accept it. When, however, he was informed by Dr. Akers that it was to be awarded upon the basis of Morrison's service to mankind he consented to receive it.

On October 18, Morrison was seen filling a role other than his usual one as an evangelist. He was in Fort Valley, Georgia, where he was to perform the ceremony, which united Miss Faith Luce and Dr. J. Kenneth Hutcherson in marriage. Little did Morrison realize then how dependent he was to become within a few weeks upon the professional skill of the young doctor whose wedding ceremony he was about to perform.

From November 7-12, 1928, Morrison preached at the North Alabama Conference of the Methodist Episcopal Church, South, in Birmingham, not knowing that this was to be his last series of meetings until May 1930. His physical condition worsened. On November 28, he was taken in an ambulance to the Deaconess Hospital in Louisville, Kentucky. The diagnosis showed a complication of bronchitis, asthma, and pleurisy. Recovery was retarded by his heart condition, which in turn was aggravated by the asthma. On January 14, his personal physician, Dr. Hutcherson, called in Dr. Emmett Horine, a well known cardiologist, for consultation. Two days later a second specialist was consulted. Morrison pleaded with the Doctors to permit him to leave Louisville and go to Florida, releasing them of all responsibility should he die on the way. On Wednesday evening, January 23, Morrison left Louisville accompanied by his wife, Dr. Kenneth Hutcherson, and the Rev. W. B. Thomas, who was serving in the capacity of a nurse. They arrived in Miami early Friday morning and Morrison was taken in an ambulance to his little bungalow, 352 N. W. 37th Street. Dr. Hutcherson remained long enough to place his patient under the care of Dr. R. O. Lyell, a local physician. Recovery was slow and it was not until April 24, 1929, that Morrison felt able to return to Kentucky.

Throughout the next eight weeks it appeared that he would soon be able to resume his evangelistic work. Early in May he attended the annual meeting of the National Holiness Association held at Asbury College. He even preached a few times. On May 28, he baptized the five children of his daughter, Mrs. Geneva Mendenhall. Five days later he preached the baccalaureate sermon for the commencement program at Asbury College. A few days following he repeated this performance at Taylor University. On June 13 he cared for some business matters in connection with the estate of his son, Howard, who died a short time before as a result of injuries suffered while serving in France during World War 1. The next day he wrote of preparations for a "Western trip"—one never made.

On June 19, Morrison was admitted to the Baptist Hospital in Louisville, where he remained until July 15. Dr. Owsley Grant, noted urologist who was called in consultation, suggested that an operation was needed, but Morrison's heart was not strong enough to permit surgery. This period of hospitalization was accompanied by great suffering, perhaps the greatest that he had ever endured.

In September a recurrence of asthma made necessary Morrison's return to the hospital—the third period of hospitalization in less than a year. His condition was so critical that he was not permitted to sit up for nearly three weeks, and, according to Morrison, on two occasions his nurse reported that he "appeared to be as near death as any patient she had ever nursed who did not die, and that both times I rallied and came back, she believes, in answer to prayer."[3]

By November recovery had been sufficient to permit traveling to Texas where the major portion of the winter was spent in the Crockett Hotel in San Antonio. An unusual period of rain and foggy weather so aggravated Morrison's cardiac asthma that at one time the attending physician told Mrs. Morrison that he expected death within a few hours. The crisis passed, however, and steady improvement followed. By January 27 the patient was able to get out of bed for a few minutes during the day, and on February 23, against the doctor's orders, he preached in the Methodist Episcopal Church, South, in San Antonio, without serious ill effects.

Dr. and Mrs. Morrison remained in San Antonio until April 8, when they traveled to Arlington, Texas, where their friend, the Rev. J. T. Upchurch, provided the Morrisons with a furnished cottage adjacent to his own residence, free of charge. He remained in Arlington until May 3, when he left with his friend Upchurch for Dallas, where they attended sessions of the General Conference. Morrison preached at least twice during this Conference. Following these meetings he returned home, arriving in Louisville on Tuesday afternoon, May 20.

Following three weeks of strenuous activity in which he participated in the Commencement programs of both Asbury College, and Taylor University, Morrison was tired and in need of rest. After spending two weeks resting and receiving treatments in the Kellogg Sanitarium, in Battle Creek, Michigan, he left feeling better than he had for many months.

When one considers the protracted illness through which Morrison had gone, his preaching schedule for the year seems remarkable. His itinerary included thirty-five separate engagements, which took him into six states. He preached before one General Conference, two Annual Conferences, and five camp meetings. In many places he spoke only once or twice, but in others he continued for a week or ten days, occasionally preaching twice a day. By November he was very tired and suffering with a recurrence of the stomach ailment, which had been troubling him intermittently for several years. From the 4th to the 25th of this month he rested and received treatments from the doctors in the Seventh Day Adventist Sanitarium in Loma Linda, California. Two strenuous revival campaigns, in Glendale and Los Angeles, California, proved too great a strain on his heart and brought him again to the verge of collapse. When on December 18 he entered the sanitarium in Paradise Valley, California, the doctor found that his pulse rate was down to forty and he was enduring great pain in his stomach. Although far from being cured, when he left the sanitarium on January 19, 1931, Morrison's health was sufficiently improved to enable him to maintain a schedule of twenty or more engagements per year throughout the next five years.

Many reasons could be given which would have justified Morrison in taking life a bit easier during the years 1931 through 1935: he had been through a term of severe illness; he had chronic heart and stomach trouble; and on March 10, 1932, he was seventy-five years of age, when one should be entitled to retirement; yet in 1933 he resumed the presidency of Asbury College, a responsibility which could easily have claimed the full time of a much younger man. In addition to this the record shows that throughout these years he filled 128 separate appointments, or an average of more than twenty-five per year. The geographic spread of his activities took him into twenty-three different states, reaching from New York and Florida in the east to Washington and California in the west, and from Mississippi in the south to Michigan in the north. From February 27 to March 3, 1934, Dr. and Mrs. Morrison joined with an evangelistic party from the Florida Fundamental Institute in a revival campaign in Havana, Cuba.

No less remarkable is the number of sermons Morrison preached and his willingness to sacrifice the comforts of home life. During 1931, the first year of evangelism after his long illness, he preached 213 times. In July 1932, he reported having spent only sixteen days and nights in his own home during the preceding nine months. He preached 290 times during the first 284 days of this same year. In June of the following year his diary records having preached 181 times in 181 days and having spent only nine nights in his own home. In his seventy-eighth year, 1934, he preached 308 sermons and spent only thirty-two nights in his home in Louisville.

Morrison had clear convictions about methods, movements, and men, and he was not afraid to express them. "One serious trouble," said Morrison while conducting a revival meeting in a Nazarene Church in Miami, Florida, "is the effort to work up a shallow emotion in the beginning of the service which is unfortunate. Singing fast songs, slapping hands, stamping feet and bringing an excitement, and pretending it is the work of the Holy Spirit is a most dangerous procedure." On another occasion he wrote that

> nothing more unfortunate has ever occurred to Methodism than the institution of "Decision Day," and the bringing of thousands of children into the church without conviction for sin, or the regeneration of the heart by the Holy Spirit. An unregenerated congregation is not a church of God.[4]

Morrison was a firm believer in the permanent contributions, which had been and were being made by the holiness camp meetings. He declared "out of these great camp meeting revivals have come the holiness schools and two or three religious denominations who emphasize in a special way the doctrine and experience of entire sanctification. They have sent their influence around the world and across the seas in the establishing of a number of missionary centers, along with an army of Spirit-filled missionaries." He was a preacher at the famous Indian Springs Camp meeting throughout a span of more than forty years. From 1930 until the time of his death he was given a standing invitation to speak there each year. The camp meeting he loved most, however, was the one he started in 1900 on land that had once been a part of his Grandfather's farm- a little distance from Glasgow, Kentucky. His fondness for this place can be seen through his activities there in June and July 1931, when he spent many days and donated nearly a thousand dollars, in building a workers' cabin, a new tabernacle and other projects of renovation on the grounds.

The panoramic presentation of the apparently vigorous evangelistic activity of this holiness preacher should not be constructed to mean that after Morrison's return to work in 1931 he enjoyed a "hale and hearty" old age. On the contrary the testimony of his journal indicates many sleepless nights because of almost continual stomach trouble, and the constant care, which was necessary to guard against over-taxing a weak heart. Many times Morrison approached the hour for service feeling so tired and weak that he wondered whether he would live to finish his sermon. Usually after beginning to speak, however, he felt something of the exhilaration, which came while as a young man he engaged in the weekly debates in Perryville, and frequently felt stronger at the close of a service than he had felt at the beginning.

While conducting a meeting in El Paso, Texas, early in 1935 during a dust storm, Morrison was overcome and was rushed in an ambulance to the Masonic Hospital where he remained from February 27 until March 4. Although he began preaching two days after his discharge from the hospital, he never completely recovered from the extra strain that had been placed upon his heart. Any unusual physical activity seemed to have dangerous repercussions. From early in January 1936, until March 22, Morrison rested in Miami, Florida. During this time he suffered much and did not feel the renewed vigor, which his winter vacations usually supplied. He spent most of his 79th birthday with his sister, Mrs. Emma Pritchard. In the evening he took a short walk and the exertion resulted in one of the most severe heart attacks he had experienced in months. It was in this weakened condition that he carried through the summer and fall schedule of five camp meetings and fifteen other engagements.

On December 1, while stopping overnight in Memphis, Tennessee, he noticed a skin irritation on his hands and face similar to that produced by poison oak. The doctors in Memphis did not seem to think the condition serious so Morrison went on to Atlanta, Georgia. Here he registered in Emory Hospital where the doctors diagnosed the ailment as asthmatic eczema. He remained in Atlanta until December 10, when upon the advice of his doctor he left for Miami, Florida, where Mrs. Morrison joined him. They lived in a rented cottage until the following March. These were months of intense suffering which time Morrison came into a new appreciation of the book of Job and the sufferings described therein.

On March 1, Dr. and Mrs. Morrison left Miami and went to Orlando where he entered the Adventist Sanitarium. The following day Mrs. Morrison returned to Louisville. He remained in the Sanitarium under doctors' care until the 29th of the month. The treatments produced some improvement, but he was still so weak that a male nurse accompanied him on the trip back to Kentucky.

During the months of April and May, Morrison rested, looked after business matters connected with the Pentecostal Publishing Company and Asbury College, and from May 2-23 preached in a revival meeting in Temple Methodist Church, Louisville. He was far from being a well man, however, and suffered much from the eczema. On June 15 he entered an Adventist Sanitarium located in Pewee Valley, about seventeen miles from Louisville, where he continued to take heat treatments until July 19. At last he found relief from the acute suffering of the preceding seven and a half months. With recovery from asthmatic eczema Morrison moved from under the dark cloud of ill health which had been hanging over him a large part of the time since the fall of 1928, and now at eighty years of age entered the final "sunset years" of his life.

Notes

[1] *The Pentecostal Herald.*

[2] Digital copy of *The Optimism of Pre-Millennialism is* freely available from First Fruits Press, along with other works of H. C. Morrison: <http://place.asburyseminary.edu/firstfruitsheritagematerial/17/>

[3] *The Pentecostal Herald.*

[4] H. C. Morrison, "Diary," 1893, 1895-1910; 1913-41.

Chapter 11
Founding Asbury Theological Seminary

Incidental reference has been made on several occasions to Asbury Theological Seminary without making further explanation. Since this institution was founded under the direct leadership of Dr. H. C. Morrison, who was its president from 1923 until 1924, and in view of its having grown until it was listed among the ten largest theological seminaries in the United States, it is appropriate that Morrison's relationship to this school should be discussed.

Throughout the first period of Morrison's administration of Asbury College the Department of Theology slowly evolved into a full-fledged theological seminary. In 1910, Morrison wanted it clearly understood that Asbury College was neither a theological seminary nor a missionary training school although throughout the years it had supplied the church with many Christian workers. He felt, however, that the number of students, who had a call to the ministry but because of age would be unable to finish both a college and a seminary program, justified the continuance of the "theological course."

In 1913 the curriculum of the Department of Theology was reorganized in order to provide two different programs. The "Certificate Course" was open only to those students who failed to meet the college entrance requirements. The "Diploma Course" was designed for college students who were concentrating on theological work rather than pursuing one of the prescribed courses leading to a degree. Many students, however, elected to take theological subjects in addition to the minimum religion requirements of the liberal arts program and thus received both a baccalaureate degree and a theological diploma. The popularity of this department was evidenced by the fact that as early as November 12, 1914, there was a sufficient number of seniors to organize a club known as the "Senior Theologians."

A distinct trend toward a thoroughly organized theological seminary can be seen in announcements made throughout the following years. In 1915 the student paper dramatically proclaimed: "A complete theological seminary course will be added to Asbury's privileges next year... This topic will receive due comment later."[1] This comment never came and the school was not started as announced, perhaps because Professor Jordan W. Carter, popular chairman of the theology department, resigned soon after Commencement in 1915.

Although Asbury College claimed to be only a liberal arts institution, by 1918 it was gaining the reputation of being a Biblical and Theological Institute as well. The trend of Morrison's thought was expressed in the following sentence: "As is seen from the curriculum, Asbury is both a College and a School of Theology, although not pretentious in her claims."[2] It was suggested that a few top-ranking seminaries in the United States were crediting some of this work toward the B. D. degree.[3]

The popularity of this department was such that by June 1920, there was a manifest need for additional dormitory and classroom space to care for the theological students, and Morrison was suggesting the necessity of another new building on the campus. In an article written for the student paper he said that he was looking to the day when there would be a graduate seminary on the campus and announced that "several courses next year...will command credit toward a postgraduate degree, provided they are not used as credits toward the A. B. degree."[4] No graduate degrees were offered during the succeeding year, but the catalogue listed, for the first time, a "School of Theology," having as its faculty H. C. Morrison, President; John H. Paul, Vice-president; Fred H. Larabee, Registrar, and Claude Lee Hawkins, Professor of Bible. It was estimated that during the years 1922-1923 two hundred students per year were preparing for the ministry in Asbury College.

The decision to found a Theological Seminary and the management of it during its early years was almost entirely a "Morrison affair." Others were interested and worked with Morrison on the original plans, but the final decisions were his. During the fall quarter of the school year, 1922-1923, George W. Ridout, F. H. Larabee, and A. P. Jones worked with Morrison on suggestions for a graduate theological school. Early in the year 1923, Morrison asked a number of the professors who were interested in this project to meet with him in his office. Plans for the proposed school were discussed thoroughly. Finally Morrison arose and in his characteristically emphatic manner declared: "Let us have it and begin with the Fall opening!"[5] This decision seems to have been the major factor in originating Asbury Theological Seminary, for no action was taken by the Board of Trustees to legally create such a school until May 31, 1926.[6] Asbury Seminary was an administrative experiment under Morrison's personal supervision.

The first printed confirmation of the plan to start a graduate school appeared on February 5, 1923, when the *New Era* carried the following notice: "The first year of theological work looking to a B. D. degree is being arranged in the catalogue for the coming year. Great interest is being shown among the ministerial students with reference to this work."[7] The announcement was carried around the world with the April 25th issue of *The Pentecostal Herald*. The College Catalogue for the following school year officially announced the offering of this course and stated "Candidates for the B. D. degree course, shall have received the degree of Bachelor of Arts from some approved College or University."[8]

Morrison's dominant influence during the first years of the Seminary is illustrated through the appointment of its first Dean. In the catalogue carrying the first announcement of the graduate theological school, F. H. Larabee was listed as Dean of both the College and the Seminary, and E. S. Guest was listed as Professor of Old Testament and Biblical Languages. Guest, however, did not receive an appointment to Asbury Theological Seminary from his Bishop and, therefore did not come. Morrison then contacted his friend, the Rev. Frank Paul Morris of Indiana and asked him to accept this professorship, which he did. Sometime later, without any Board action, Dr. Morrison simply said to Professor Morris, "I want you to be Dean, prepare a course of study." Concerning this year's experience Morris later said, "I bore the name of Dean, but had no office, had no money to spend on a catalogue and did none of the things which the office of Dean now takes care of...I suppose I could be called 'Acting' Dean, since someone had to bear the name." The following year, after F. P. Morris' name had been printed in the Catalogue as Dean, he was asked to step aside in favor of F. H. Larabee in order that some other changes advantageous to the College program might be made—a request to which Morris acceded with gentlemanly grace.[9]

The evolution of Asbury Theological Seminary into an independent legally incorporated school required a span of several years. The next step after the founding of the Seminary upon the authority of Dr. Morrison was the quasi-recognition of its existence by the action of the Board of Trustees through the appointment of F. H. Larabee as Dean—an action taken at Morrison's request. In May 1925, the Executive Committee of the Board of Trustees of Asbury College recommended a change in the Articles of Incorporation which would permit the establishment of a Theological Seminary with a separate theological faculty and the right to grant degrees, but for some reason the recommendation was not presented to the Board of Trustees during the annual meeting the following month. Actions were taken, however, which assumed the existence of the Seminary. It was during this meeting that Morrison resigned as President of Asbury College. When L. R. Akers was elected as his successor the executive leadership of the Seminary was not included. Morrison was elected as President of Asbury Theological Seminary and Dr. F. P. Morris as Vice-President. At an adjourned meeting of the Board, Morris' name was withdrawn and Akers was elected to that office.[10]

It was not until the annual meeting of the Board of Trustees on May 31, 1926, that the Seminary was given legal status through the adoption of a resolution authorizing the establishment of a separate school to be known as *Asbury Theological Seminary*. This school was to have authority to maintain its separate faculty and to grant appropriate theological degrees, though ultimate control remained in the Board of Trustees of Asbury College.[11]

Asbury Theological Seminary continued to work in close co-operation with Asbury College, and remained under the control of its Board of Trustees for another five years. It was not until 1929 that the listing of the Seminary courses of study were discontinued as a part of the College Catalogue. Following Morrison's long and severe illness in 1929-1930 his burden for the success of the Seminary increased. Although at this time Morrison Hall was furnishing adequate housing facilities for the growing student body of the Seminary, the enterprise had almost no financial foundation. He felt that greater economic self-sufficiency could be achieved through complete independence from Asbury College.

Throughout the closing days of May 1931, Morrison worked with a committee in planning a charter for Asbury Theological Seminary. On June 1, the Board of Trustees of Asbury College gave authorization for the drawing up of such a paper with the stipulation that certain measures be included to perpetuate adherence to theological doctrines, which were held as sacred by the members of the Board.

> *Resolved*, that this Board instruct, Dr. H. C. Morrison with a selected committee to prepare a charter for Asbury Theological Seminary, said charter to be in strict harmony with the Constitution of Asbury College.
>
> This charter shall lay special emphasis upon the divine inspiration of the Holy Scripture, the Virgin Birth, Mediatorial Death and Bodily Resurrection of our Lord Jesus Christ, placing special emphasis upon the necessity of the regeneration of the individual and entire sanctification subsequent to regeneration as taught by John Wesley and the founders of Methodism.
>
> This charter shall be so drawn as to guard positively against every form of modern

liberalism and shall be submitted for the approval of this Board.[12]

Little time was lost in activating the authority thus given, for on June 4, 1931, the Articles of Incorporation of Asbury Theological Seminary were signed by ten persons acting as incorporators.[13] With the signing of this charter Asbury Theological Seminary became an independent and legally organized institution. On the first Tuesday of June 1932, the incorporators met and completed the organization in harmony with the regulations as originally outlined. The ensuing election of officers resulted in the selection of H. C. Morrison, President of both the Board of Trustees and of the Seminary; Robert H. Williams, Vice-President; Frank P. Morris, Secretary; and Mrs. H. C. Morrison, Treasurer.[14] Morrison continued to hold the office of president throughout the remainder of his life.

An elaborate discussion of the history of Christian thought in America is outside the province of this study, but some reference must be made to certain trends of theological development in order to understand Morrison's purpose in founding another theological seminary. From the early days of colonial America until well into the nineteenth century, religion in America was founded upon a basic Biblicism. Immediately after the Civil War two diverse trends appeared: the conservatives, producing both the "holiness revival" and the "fundamentalists" and the "liberals" or "modernists," who have become predominant in America Protestantism.[15]

The "holiness revival" developed much earlier in the North than in the South. In 1867 the "National Association for the Promotion of Holiness" was organized under the leadership of William B. Osbourne, John S. Inskip, and J. A. Wood— Methodist ministers. While there was a residual belief in the doctrine, especially within the Methodist Episcopal Church,

South, the evangelistic fervor of the movement did not affect the South with great force until after 1876. During the summer of that year the Rev. A. J. Jarrell of St. James Methodist Church, Augusta, Georgia, attended one of the National Holiness Camp Meetings, at Ocean Grove, New Jersey, and there accepted sanctification. He then engaged the Rev. John Inskip to hold a revival in his church in Augusta. This led to other holiness revival meetings being held in the South. As the movement spread during the remaining years of the nineteenth century it produced the religious environment which greatly affected the lives of men like Morrison and J. W. Hughes, as a result of which Asbury College was organized. Although the issues related to the "holiness revival" were not the major factors in stimulating the organization of Asbury Theological Seminary they should not be disregarded, for the doctrine of entire sanctification has always been a vital theological tenet advocated by this organization.

The spread of "liberalism" and its reaction movement, "fundamentalism," progressed slowly during the latter part of the nineteenth century but gained increasing momentum in the first two decades of the twentieth. The increasing influence of theological liberalism continued until "practically all well-known seminaries in the North (except Princeton) experienced a liberalizing conversion, in spite of the effort of orthodox leaders to keep them in accord with their historic testimony."[16] The results of a survey of 700 pastors and theological students made by G. H. Betts showed that by 1928 the only point upon which these Protestant ministers were able to agree was "that God exists." As one might expect, the theological students departed more widely from the doctrines of traditional orthodoxy than did the older ministers. Only thirty-three percent of the younger men held the New Testament to be an absolute standard of religious belief. Only five percent adhered to the story of creation as recounted in Genesis, and seventy-five percent held that the Bible was written as a result of a type of inspiration no different from that used in the production of any other great religious book. Only one tenth of the young men considered that belief in the virgin birth of Jesus, participation in any sacraments, or church membership was essential to salvation.[17] Regardless of the relative value of the various views held, these replies indicated a distinct shift from the orthodox position of 1900.

The conservatives were not inactive throughout these years, even though they were gradually losing control of the larger Protestant denominations. Many Bible and prophetic conferences were sponsored by this group, chief of which were those held in Niagara, New York; Winona Lake, Indiana; and Denver, Colorado. In 1895 the Niagara group set forth the famous "five points of fundamentalism" which they insisted should be universally accepted by all Christians. Large quantities of literature, of varying degrees of scholarship, were disseminated, the most noted of which was the publication of twelve small volumes beginning in 1909, known as *The Fundamentals*. In 1919, the World Christian Fundamentals Association was organized under the leadership of W. B. Riley and A. C. Dixon. Enthusiastic members conducted conventions throughout the country in which they attacked the proponents of Biblical "higher criticism" and of Darwinian evolution.

The struggle between the forces of liberalism and fundamentalism was reflected by the changing emphasis in articles published in Morrison's paper, *The Pentecostal Herald*. Prior to 1900 the emphasis was on examination and presentation of the doctrine of Entire Sanctification as being both Biblical and representative of the true teaching of early Methodism. Twenty years later its pages were filled with articles demonstrating a conservative reaction to the liberal trend in theology. From 1921 to 1923 *The Pentecostal Herald* attacked religious liberalism in a vigorous manner. On November 2, 1921, a special "Battling for the Bible" issue was published in which there were featured articles by William Jennings Bryan, and Harold Paul Sloan, editor of the New York *Christian Advocate*. On April 26, 1922, the emphasis was placed on "Christian Fundamentals," and the influence of Bishop W. A. Candler of the Methodist Episcopal Church, South, was added to the list of authors making a contribution. In climaxing the campaign, Morrison wrote a long series of "Open Letters to Rev. Harry Emerson Fosdick" in which he attacked the teachings of the eminent New York City minister as being representative of the liberal theological trend of the time.

It was in 1923, when the "Modernist-Fundamentalist" controversy was at its peak, that Asbury Theological Seminary was founded. The reasons given for its organization and the statements of its doctrinal position clearly reflect the influence of that tumultuous theological era. "Twenty-five years ago," Morrison wrote, "it seemed to be the special work of the holiness movement to proclaim full salvation to believers, but now their sphere of labor has become greatly enlarged, and they must contend for all the fundamental doctrines of the Bible, yea, for the inspiration of the Bible itself."[18]

This concern for the preservation of the historic teachings of John Wesley and of early Methodism was expressed in the first *Bulletin of Asbury Theological Seminary*, 1923-1924:

> There are many schools of Theology to which they [theological students] might go, but the danger points are many, and there are not a few church schools where the Evangelical faith and Evangelistic fervor of students are both shattered and destroyed very soon after their entrance and they are taught in an atmosphere

absolutely detrimental to the Christian faith as set forth in the Holy Scriptures and in the Church's Articles of Religion. As a consequence young men are graduating from these schools and going into pulpits preaching Modernism instead of Christian Faith, skepticism instead of Divine Assurance, human creeds and systems instead of the whole Counsel of God.[19]

As an antidote for the liberalism so prevalent at the time, Asbury Seminary presented its affirmation of faith:

> Asbury Theological Seminary regards it fundamental to maintain in all its teachings and doctrines of the faith which have come down to us from the Apostles and the Fathers, the faith that has been tested through the ages, the faith that gave birth to the Reformation and that in the latter days brought on the great Evangelical Revival in the days of John Wesley. All our teachings will range around the Bible as an inspired book; around the Cross as the great center of Redemption's plan; around Jesus Christ as the Incarnate Son of God who died the just for the unjust that he might bring us unto God. In these days of tragic unbelief we must build a School of Theology at Asbury where Divinity students will grow in Faith and Grace as well as in intellectual attainments, and where they can acquire a sound Theological training consistent with a sound Gospel faith.

> Asbury stands for the Arminian-Wesleyan Faith which believes in the Triune God, the Trinity, in Divine Revelation, in Inspired Scriptures – their sufficiency of truth—the Fall of Man, the Incarnation, the Divine Christ, the Atonement for Sin, Pardon, Regeneration and Sanctification by Faith, The Second Coming of Christ, The Judgment, Heaven and Hell.[20]

Morrison's zeal as a proponent of evangelical Christianity had not abated when, in 1931, he was the dominating personality on a committee, which drew up the Articles of Incorporation of Asbury Theological Seminary. The objective of the corporation was stated as being:

> To maintain the corporation as a Theological Seminary for the promotion of Theological Education. It will be the subject of this Seminary to prepare and send forth a well-trained, sanctified, Spirit-filled, Evangelistic Ministry. This Seminary will emphasize in its teaching the divine inspiration and infallibility of the Holy Scripture, the Virgin Birth, Godhead, Vicarious Sufferings, and bodily resurrection of our Lord Jesus Christ. The instruction of this Seminary will fully recognize the fallen estate of mankind, the necessity of individual regeneration, the witness of the Spirit, the remains of the carnal nature, and entire sanctification as a definite second work of grace subsequent to regeneration. The instruction of this Seminary will conform fully to the Wesleyan interpretation of Scripture. The instructors in this institution will guard with

> jealous care against any sort of teaching in sympathy with modern liberalism.[21]

No person was to hold any official position in the corporation or on the teaching staff who was out of harmony with the basic doctrines as listed. As a further guard against deviation from these objectives the Articles provided that should the institution ever repudiate these standards in any way, all donors to the school, or their heirs, would be entitled to full repayment for all gifts.[22]

This purpose of maintaining a Theological Seminary which would guard against the teachings of modernistic liberalism on the one hand and strong Calvinism on the other, while at the same time providing a training in "evangelical Christianity as interpreted by historic Wesleyan theology," remained constant throughout the life of Morrison—and to the present time (1963).

Although the incorporation of the Seminary in 1931 made it an institution legally separate from Asbury College, there continued to be a close affinity between the two schools for a number of years. For some time they continued to operate on the same campus. From 1933 to 1940 H. C. Morrison was president of both institutions, and for a large part of this time, because of the financial exigency, they were operated on the same budget. This was less difficult than it would at first appear for there was a very large overlapping in the personnel of the two Boards of Trustees. A similar interchange was to be found in curriculum and teaching staff.

One of the measures taken to bring about separation of the two institutions was the decision to enlarge the Seminary curriculum to a full three-year program of graduate study. This program was put into operation in the fall of 1937. For the first time the schools were operating with independent curricula.

For several years Asbury College had been striving to become an accredited member of the Southern Association of Colleges, Universities, and Secondary Schools. One of the final steps necessary to achieve this goal was a complete separation in the operation of the College and the Seminary. This necessitated the moving of the Seminary to a separate campus. Arrangements were made to rent the Talbott Hotel building, then in the process of construction as a part of the College endowment program, to Asbury Theological Seminary for use as an administration building. Thus in September 1939, Asbury Theological Seminary opened its doors on a new campus. For the first time the two schools were independent as to legal corporation, curriculum, teaching staff, location, and operation.

Although this move was of great benefit to the College, it meant real sacrifice on the part of the Seminary. The separation of the two schools meant relinquishing all claims to any property on the campus of Asbury College; therefore the Seminary became a school possessing neither endowment funds nor real estate. Throughout 1940 a number of appeals were made through the pages of *The Herald* for money with which to buy property and construct adequate buildings for the Seminary.

With its separation from Asbury College the suggestion arose of relocating the Seminary. In 1940 "the Executive Committee, together with Mrs. H. C. Morrison, J. L. Piercy, T. D. Crary, and S. H. Turbeville, were constituted a committee with power to act to investigate the possibility of moving the Seminary to Louisville, Kentucky."[23] Before any definite action was taken by this group, however, Dr. Z. T. Johnson and the Board of Trustees of Asbury College made a proposal. While the two schools had been operating together, funds designated for the Seminary had been invested in property now located on the campus of the College. It was felt that as a consequence the College had a moral if not a legal obligation to make some settlement. The Board of Trustees of Asbury College voted to give the Talbott Hotel to Asbury Theological Seminary in full settlement for "all claims the Seminary might have against the College for Morrison Hall and all other matters."[24] This transaction settled the problem of location for Asbury Theological Seminary—it was to remain in Wilmore.

One more step was necessary to make the separation complete. On April 21, 1942, Dr. Johnson received a letter from the Executive Secretary of the Southern Association of Colleges, Universities and Secondary Schools containing a recommendation that the overlapping of trustees in the two institutions be discontinued.[25] Special committees were appointed by the Boards of Trustees of the two schools to study the problem. As a result those who were members of both Boards voluntarily resigned from one Board or the other and new members were elected to fill the vacancies until by October 24, 1942, the overlapping of personnel had been obliterated and the final separation of the two institutions was effected.[26]

If increase in student enrollment is a measure of the need for a school then Morrison must have felt some justification for having founded Asbury Theological Seminary. Although it was said that Asbury College had two hundred students training for the ministry in 1922-1923, only three were registered as *bona fide* graduate students in the newly organized Seminary the following fall. The records show an increase each year until there were sixty-two students during the school year 1929-1930. Succeeding years displayed some fluctuation but the trend was toward a larger student body. The peak enrollment in the history of the school to that date was obtained in 1941-1942—the year of Morrison's death—a total of eighty-nine. Through the commencement of 1942, the B.D. degree had been granted to 226 persons, and many times that number have been graduated since then.

The long struggle to receive academic recognition for the work done in Asbury Theological Seminary provides another interesting chapter in the history of its development. During its first year, when the reaction to liberalism was strong, Morrison said that no recognition would be asked of any group in any way friendly to the liberal higher critics.

The question of accreditation was rising as early as 1932, however, even though at that time the Seminary graduates were being widely accepted throughout Methodism, as well as by other ecclesiastical bodies. By 1936 enough criticism had arisen to cause Dean Larabee to recommend that the acceptance of undergraduate work be discontinued and the curriculum be arranged on the basis of three full years of graduate study as soon as sufficient funds were available to provide an adequate faculty. Although the program at Asbury Seminary was in harmony with that practiced by Southern seminaries, such as Duke and Emory, it was being criticized by some of the Northern and Eastern Schools. The following year the Board of Trustees voted to inaugurate the three year program.

A new problem arose in 1939 after the union of the three great Methodist bodies into one church. The Uniting Conference of the Methodist Church created the University Senate as an accrediting and standardizing agency for all educational institutions connected with Methodism. It also approved or disapproved the work of other schools seeking to train candidates for the Methodist ministry. It was a severe blow to Asbury Theological Seminary when accreditation by the American Association of Theological Schools was proclaimed as one of the pre-requisites to acceptance by the University

Senate. Although originally distasteful to Morrison, the quest for accreditation by the American Association of Theological Schools seemed the best of any of the alternatives suggested.

Asbury Theological Seminary had first become a member of the American Association of Theological Schools in 1937, but from 1939 until 1946 constant efforts were made to meet the standards of the Association for accreditation. This goal was not achieved during the life of Morrison for in 1939 the school was without buildings, endowment, a library worthy of the name, or a faculty of sufficient size to offer an adequate course of study. The application made during the school year 1941-1942 was not approved because of the Seminary's failure to meet endowment qualifications.[27] Efforts in this endeavor continued unabated after Morrison's death until the goal was finally achieved and Asbury Theological Seminary was accepted on June 11, 1946, as a fully accredited member of the American Association of Theological Schools. Early in 1947 the Seminary was placed by the University Senate on the list of schools approved for the training of young men for the Methodist ministry.

Morrison's interest in the training of young ministers deepened after his severe illness in 1929-1930, into what seemed, to him at least, to be a divine commission. "I am hoping to be able to preach the gospel, if He should extend my life, for some years yet," Morrison wrote in March 1930, "but it occurs to me that if my Lord has raised me up for a purpose, that purpose is to build up and enlarge the scope of Asbury Theological Seminary, Wilmore, Kentucky. As never before, I hope to devote such energy as God may give me, to this great work."[28] Throughout the five years, while serving as President of both Asbury College and Asbury Seminary the burden of liquidating the stupendous debt of the College was so great that the needs of the Seminary could not be stressed, though they were mentioned along with those of the College. In 1938, however, after those financial obligations had been met, he turned his interest to the Seminary once more.

In what proved to be his last appeal for Asbury Theological Seminary, Morrison referred to his "call" to build such a school. He felt that all of his previous activity had been a preparation for this final and greatest responsibility of his life. He concluded by saying:

> I should not undertake the building of this Seminary, but for the fact that I feel it is one of the greatest needs in the world; that we should have a Theological Seminary in teaching and purpose, in perfect accord with the spirit and message of John Wesley and his co-workers, in the kindling of the greatest religious revival in the history of the Christian Church.[29]

Morrison felt a responsibility not only to provide a school for the training of young people but also to provide the necessary funds to enable them to attend the school. From early in 1922 until the closing months of 1928 he made frequent appeals for contributions to what he termed the "student loan fund." His desire was to have a revolving fund of at least $25,000, which could be loaned to worthy students at four percent interest.

On June 29, 1932, a scholarship program was proposed as a substitute for the loan fund. A scholarship of ninety-five dollars would pay the tuition and fees for one student for an entire school year. Within a short time enough money had been provided for several scholarships. The policy of mutually identifying both donor and recipient of the scholarship increased the interest for both. Approximately $12,000 was raised for this purpose during the next two years, largely through the efforts of Dr. and Mrs. Morrison. In subsequent years it has grown to many times this amount.

H. C. Morrison's interest in the perpetuation of Asbury Theological Seminary and in the training of ministerial students was such that he made provision for the continuation of the work after his death. One of the clauses of his will stated that the Pentecostal Publishing Company should be placed under the control of "The Morrison Theological Trust." The purpose of this organization is:

> To provide funds for the use and benefit of such educational institution or institutions as prepare for the ministry wholly sanctified young men, all this with the purpose and view that there shall thereby be aided promulgation of the fundamental tenets of the Christian faith of absolute loyalty to the Holy Scriptures, Old Testament and New, as interpreted and taught by John Wesley, embracing the fall and sinfulness of the human race, repentance, saving faith in Christ, regeneration and the witness of the Spirit, the fact of remaining sin in the believers, and of entire sanctification by consecration and faith.[30]

Since its organization the assets of this company have been listed as $300,000 of the endowment funds of Asbury Theological Seminary.

The sudden death of Dr. H. C. Morrison on March 24, 1942, left Asbury Theological Seminary without a president and with no immediate plans for a permanent successor. On April 3, at a special called meeting of the Board of Trustees, Julian C. McPheeters, pastor of the Glide Memorial Methodist Church at

San Francisco, California, was elected Acting-President to serve until the regular meeting of the Board of Trustees. In June 1942, he was duly elected President of the Seminary and served in that office until his retirement on May 28, 1962. The measure of success achieved by Asbury Theological Seminary since 1942 is a tribute, in part at least, to the vision and work of H. C. Morrison, founder and first President of the school.

Notes

[1] *Asbury College New Era.*

[2] *Catalogue of Asbury College.*

[3] *Ibid.*

[4] *Asbury College New Era.*

[5] *The Pentecostal Herald.*

[6] "Minutes of the Annual Meeting of the Board of Trustees of Asbury College."

[7] *Asbury College New Era.*

[8] *Catalogue of Asbury College.*

[9] Letter from Frank Paul Morris, to Paul Abel, Sept. 7, 1950.

[10] "Minutes of the Annual Meeting of the Board of Trustees of Asbury College."

[11] *Ibid.*

[12] *Ibid.*

[13] "Articles of Incorporation of Asbury Theological Seminary."

[14] H. C. Morrison, "Diary," 1893, 1895-1910; 1913-41.

[15] Merrill E. Gaddis, "Christian Perfectionism in America" (Unpublished Ph. D. Thesis, University of Chicago, 1929).

[16] W. W. Sweet, *Methodism in American History* (Chicago, 1933). Hereafter referred to as *Methodism in American History.*

[17] Winfred Ernest Garrison, *The March of Faith* (New York, 1933).

[18] H. C. Morrison, *Open Letters to the Bishops, Ministers, and Members of the Methodist Episcopal Church, South* (Louisville, n. d.). Hereafter referred to as *Open Letters to the Bishops*.

[19] *Bulletin of Asbury Theological Seminary.*

[20] *Ibid.*

[21] "Articles of Incorporation of Asbury Theological Seminary."

[22] *Ibid.*

[23] "Minute Records of the Board of Trustees of Asbury Theological Seminary." Hereafter referred to as "Board of Trustees Minutes."

[24] *Ibid.*

[25] *Ibid.*

[26] "Board of Trustees Minutes."

[27] *Ibid.*

[28] *The Pentecostal Herald.*

[29] *Ibid.*

[30] *The Christian Advocate.*

Chapter 12
Sunset Years

H. C. Morrison celebrated his eightieth birthday by preaching in the chapel of the Seventh Day Adventist Sanitarium in Orlando, Florida. One would expect that after having lived and labored through fourscore years Morrison would retire from strenuous service, or at least limit his activities to those considered commensurate to one of his age. Such was not to be the case, however. Previous discussion has already told of his activity as editor of *The Pentecostal Herald* up to the close of his life; of his relationship to Asbury College as its president until 1940; and of his active leadership in Asbury Theological Seminary until 1942. In addition to these heavy responsibilities, Morrison continued his work of evangelism to the very end.

Although sickness kept him from active service during the first four months of 1937, throughout the remainder of the year he preached 233 times, in thirteen different meetings, which took him into eight states. Throughout the eighty-second year of his life (March 10, 1938—March 10, 1939) Morrison delivered 368 sermons. In doing this he traveled 15,000 miles in thirteen states and spoke to audiences which he estimated to total 20,000 persons. In April, 1938, he served as a ministerial delegate from the Kentucky Conference to the General Conference of the Methodist Episcopal Church, South, meeting in Birmingham, Alabama. This was the seventh time he had served in this capacity.

The succeeding two years showed no abatement in his schedule. Fifty-two meetings were conducted during this period. Fifteen of these were camp meetings, calling for the extra energy usual to that type of preaching. Throughout the calendar years 1938 and 1939, Morrison preached 391 times each year. Even with so strenuous a schedule he seemed to remain in comparatively good health—only five feet eight inches tall he maintained a weight of 186 pounds. He spent only twenty-two nights in his own home during the year 1939, and addressed 365 audiences during the first 319 days of the year. The testimony he gave on his eighty-fourth birthday portrays not only his work, but also something of his spirit as a venerable old man.

> Here I am at my eighty-fourth birthday. A glance at the passing years, and life seems very short; thinking over the various periods, the various experiences in different fields of service, and it seems like a long stretch of years.
>
> Looking backward, there is much to be thankful for, much to regret, and nothing to boast of. I think with gratitude of the countless mercies of God, his patience with an unworthy servant, and go forward singing, "Nothing in my hand I bring; simply to thy cross I cling."
>
> Consulting my diary I find in my eighty-fourth year I preached 38 times, in 13 states, traveled 3,000 miles by auto, 800 miles by bus and about 13,000 by train. It has been a busy year, but a blessed year. I have seen hundreds of souls at the altar of prayer, and quite a number have

> been regenerated or sanctified, others blessed and strengthened for their task.
>
> I believe with all my heart the gospel I have preached; would that I had preached it better. I adore Jesus Christ and have tried to proclaim him to my fellow beings as one mighty to save to the uttermost. I long to serve him more faithfully, and ask the prayers of *The Herald* family that I may "be found faithful in him, not having spot or wrinkle, or any such thing." As the evening shadows lengthen I long to respond to some calls for meetings in dear old Kentucky.[1]

The pace was slackened only slightly during 1941, the last full year of his life. On the closing day of the year the record in his diary shows that he had preached 274 times. Of the twenty-four meetings conducted by Morrison, twenty-one continued for five days or more. Only twelve nights were spent in his own home in Louisville throughout this entire period. He averaged twenty-four revival campaigns per year during the five years following his eightieth birthday—a record comparable to that of any similar period throughout his evangelistic career. In the Annual Conference of 1941 Morrison received appointment from the Bishop to the Presidency of Asbury Theological Seminary. Concerning this Morrison said: "I suppose I am the oldest man receiving appointment and in active service, in Methodism, and perhaps the oldest editor in active service in the world..."[2]

Morrison retained his vision and courage for the undertaking of new projects throughout the sunset of his life. In December 1937 he felt that there was need for another holiness camp meeting in Florida. He found a forty acre tract of land near Sebring which seemed suitable for the purpose. The tract was purchased by John Taylor, Charles Lanier, and H. C. Morrison, and was added to Asbury College for the purpose of establishing a holiness camp meeting. Morrison envisioned a large campground with a circular drive, large tabernacle, dining hall, workers' cottage, and many privately owned cottages on the ground. In his mind it was to be developed into a place where retired ministers would build their homes and where Bishops and other church leaders could find a quiet haven for rest.

Within a few days after the purchase of the property Morrison personally supervised cleaning up the grounds, laying off the circular drive and planting palm trees. From December 19, 1939, until January 12, 1940, and again from January 23 until February 1, he spent many days of what was to have been his vacation in supervising the construction of a dining hall and workers' cottage. Necessary furniture was purchased and placed in the buildings. Fruit trees, Australian Pines, and 200 feet of hedge were all set out by a landscaping company. The expense for this was largely cared for from Morrison's personal funds, and given as a donation to Asbury College.

The first services were held on the John Wesley Park Holiness Campground from February 2-11, 1940. No tabernacle had been erected but services were held in a tent. Attendance was considered to be as large as could be expected for the first year of a new camp meeting, and prospects for the future seemed very hopeful. The next year, however, no regular camp meeting was held, though Morrison used the dining hall as an auditorium and preached six times in March, 1941. No mention of this camp meeting appeared in the record of Morrison's activities during the early months of 1942, thus leaving one with the impression that his visionary program did not materialize as he had anticipated.

Even as an octogenarian Morrison did not lose interest in the temporal affairs of this life. After having seen the beautiful log house which his friend, the Rev. J. L. Piercy, had built a short distance outside of Glasgow, Kentucky, Morrison knew that he would never be satisfied until he had one as good or better. As a result he purchased a beautifully wooded tract of two and a half acres near Glasgow. He arranged with his friend Piercy to supervise the building of the house which he had planned. Construction was started early in 1937 and continued in a spasmodic manner until November, 1938. In the intervals between revival campaigns Morrison made more than twenty trips to Glasgow to check on the progress which was being made. He seemed to take great pleasure in the work and in looking forward to having a large, comfortable place where he could live and find the peace and quiet necessary to do some writing.

When the building was finally completed it was indeed something to be desired! The two story log house, placed some distance from the road, and surrounded by numbers of shade trees, presented a picture of restful retreat. The seven room house had four bedrooms, each with its own fireplace and private bath. It is little wonder that Morrison said of it: "I have longed for a house and home of my own. Where I could have warmth and some real rest."[3]

Morrison's dream of retirement and rest never materialized. According to information gleaned from his diaries he actually spent less than two weeks in his Glasgow home. Furniture was first placed in the house on July 13, 1938 and Morrison stayed there until July 19. Two of his daughters, Anna Laura and Helen, spent the week-end with him there—the largest family gathering to live in the house. He did not return again until June 9, 1939, when he spent one night there and reported having had a "good rest." A week later he enjoyed the restful atmosphere of his home for a part of one day, but was unable to stay over night since he was engaged in a revival campaign in Scottsville, Kentucky, where J. L. Piercy was the pastor. One year later Morrison and his daughter, Anna Laura Young, spent four days in Glasgow, June 18-21. These could hardly be described as days of rest, however, for during that time he wrote several chapters in his book, *Some Chapters of My Life Story*, as well as several sermons. Aside from the two brief visits of only a few hours each during which he was arranging for the care of the property, he never visited the house again.

As the years slipped by and Morrison outlived his friends of former days an increasing sense of loneliness came to him. "My mind oft turns back with a bit of longing," he said in 1938, "for the friends and loved ones of other days. So many of them have passed away. If I were not in love with Jesus Christ and busy in His service I would grow lonely."[4] His pattern of hurried activity continued, however, to the end of his life. In spite of frequent trips across the country, his visit to his daughter Emily (Mrs. Douglas Chandler) in June, 1938, was the first time he had seen her in seven years. When his only sister, Emma, died on May 21, 1940, he was so much involved in the struggle over the presidency of Asbury College that he did not take time to attend the funeral.

His increasing age was accompanied by a tendency to indulge in reminiscence and by a mellowing of spirit — frequently characteristic of those whose locks have grown white with the passing of years. On the pages of some of his diaries there was found written, in a manner akin to doodling, the name, date of birth, date of marriage and date of death of his second wife, Geneva Pedlar Morrison. It seemed indicative of a deep affection that was rising again as the experiences of the past were being relieved in the halls of memory. His dynamic, authoritative manner had not vanished, but his spirit was much more mellow than it had been in his more youthful years. One diary entry indicates there was more willingness to recognize his weakness: "I grieved the brethren a little by cutting short the singing. I had better kept quiet but there is such a tendency to keep on and on, waste time. The Lord help me to keep quiet- to suffer long and be kind."[5] On another occasion he recorded a humble testimony: "Looking backward I am amazed at the patient mercy of God to me. I grieve that I have not been more faithful. Thank God for His compassion and long suffering. I should be very patient and forgiving to others."[6] As the weariness of years rested more heavily upon him he expressed his desire for eternal rest: "I find a sweet willingness in my heart to leave all the things for which I have labored, and loved in the hands of God and to go to my Savior's feet and rest. It is a most comfortable feeling."[7]

In January, 1942, John Paul described Morrison's physical condition by saying, "Thousands will be interested to know that Dr. H. C. Morrison reappeared as his old self in White City Camp [Avon Park, Florida]. ...He seemed carefree, youthful in spirit and preached his best in many years."[8] After participating in four other revival campaigns Morrison went on March 21, 1942, to Elizabethton, Tennessee, where he was to assist the Rev. Solon McNeese, pastor of the First Methodist Church, in a series of meetings. On Monday, March 23, he appropriately preached what proved to be his valedictory sermon on the topic, "How to Win a Sinner to Christ," the theme of his sixty-three and one-half years in the ministry. The pastor gave an account of the unusual closing of this service.

> After the service had closed, the people did not wish to go. Dr. Morrison started that great old hymn: "What a Friend We Have in Jesus." He sang a verse, the choir picked it up, and then

> the congregation joined in. It sounded like the singing of angels to me. Dr. Morrison then asked: "How many people in this vast gathering have a friend or loved one you are going to help win to Christ?" Practically every hand went up. We sang another verse. Then he said, "I feel like praying" and knelt by the pulpit. He ended his prayer by thanking God for that beautiful scene. "Here is this great throng of people saying they will do their best to win someone to Christ. Lord, help them to make good, one hundred percent. Amen." After singing again, he dismissed the congregation a second time. They were loathe to go. Many handkerchiefs were lifted—people wiping tears from their eyes. In his characteristic way, Dr. Morrison said: "You may run along now!" *That was his last service on earth.*"[9]

The following morning, March 4, the pastor stopped at the hotel to take Morrison to the morning service, but found him unable to go as he was suffering with an attack of asthma. A doctor was summoned and Morrison responded to treatment. By noon he appeared as well as usual, and upon the insistence of Rev. Mr. McNeese he wrote a letter to his wife. It was thought best to move Morrison from the hotel to the parsonage, but before they left the room that afternoon Morrison prayed the following prayer:

> Lord, you understand my case. You know why I'm here and what the opportunity is. I'll appreciate it very much, Lord, if you will let me finish this meeting. Lord, I'll appreciate it very much if you will let me return to Louisville, Ky., and see my wife once more; and Lord, there are

two or three little business matters that I want
to attend to. If you will let me do these things,
Lord, it will be right then for me to go. But if
you do not see fit in your infinite wisdom to
grant this prayer, it will be all right. Amen.[10]

Morrison ate his dinner at six o'clock that evening and appeared in his usual health. By seven he seemed nervous and anxious to get to the service. After failing to persuade Morrison to take the evening off for rest, McNeese took him to the church, arriving a little before eight o'clock. By this time Morrison was again having difficulty with his breathing but said, "If I could get into the pulpit I would have supernatural power...to throw this off." He did not go into the church, however, and a few minutes later said, "McNeese if you take me into the church I'll die."

They returned to the parsonage where a physician was summoned. Following about fifty minutes of intense suffering some relief was obtained. The physician realized that the treatment was not producing the desired reaction and returned to his office to get a different medicine. While the doctor was gone Morrison seemed to rally and asked McNeese to pray. During the prayer Morrison responded with "Amen" and other indications of his assent. At its conclusion he said, "I feel much better and I'm all right." McNeese walked across the room to make an adjustment in the light. When he turned again he saw Morrison's head gradually resting on his left shoulder. "His heart stopped. He was *gone!* Not a sigh. Not a struggle. I never saw mortal man die easier. God came and took His friend and went away."[11]

After being pronounced dead by the physician, his body was removed to the Roy Hathaway Funeral Home where it was prepared for burial. The following day a memorial service was held in the First Methodist Church in Elizabethton before Morrison's body was taken to Wilmore, Kentucky.

Funeral services were held for H. C. Morrison in Hughes Auditorium of Asbury College on the afternoon of March 27, 1942. The Rev. M. C. Yates, pastor of the Wilmore Methodist church was in charge. The Scripture lesson was read by Dr. Z. T. Johnson and prayer was offered by Dr. L. R. Akers. Following the account of Morrison's last hours by the Rev. Solon McNeese, tributes to Morrison were given by Dr. W. L. Clark, Dr. Paul S. Rees, Dr. Ira N. Hargett, and Bishop U. V. W. Darlington. Following a quartet rendition of the song, "No Night There," internment was made, during a downpour of rain, in the cemetery at Wilmore, Kentucky. The life and work of Henry Clay Morrison, the "Crusader Saint" was ended, but his influence continues to live on.

Notes

[1] *The Pentecostal Herald.*

[2] *Ibid.*

[3] H. C. Morrison, "Diary," 1893, 1895-1910; 1913-41.

[4] *Ibid.*

[5] *Ibid.*

[6] H *Ibid.*

[7] *Ibid.*

[8] *The Pentecostal Herald.*

[9] H. C. Morrison, "Diary," 1893, 1895-1910; 1913-41.

[10] *The Pentecostal Herald.*

[11] Stenographic record of statements made at the funeral of H. C. Morrison. Hereafter referred to as "Stenographic Records."

Chapter 13
Theological Emphasis

Henry Clay Morrison was a preacher not a research scholar; he was a crusading-warrior, not a theologian. To attempt to present a systematic theology from a man who neither thought nor acted according to such a pattern would be futile. It would be unfair, however, to close the life story of a man whose major contribution to the world was made through his activity as a religious "crusading-warrior" without presenting some summary statements of the theological convictions for which he was willing to give battle. The purpose of this chapter is to present some of his doctrinal tenets: Entire Sanctification, Reaction to Modernism, Bibliology, Christology, Eschatology, and social teachings.

An attempt will be made to gather and present in an organized form some of the major theological emphases which have been alluded to previously. Insofar as possible, Morrison will be allowed to speak for himself. The order of presentation cannot be the logical arrangement usually followed by the professional theologian, but is rather an attempt to present a montage of Morrison's theological opinions.

Entire Sanctification

The stress which Morrison placed upon the doctrine of entire sanctification must not be construed to mean that he minimized the fundamental doctrine of regeneration or conversion. After forty years as editor of *The Pentecostal Herald* he still expressed his belief in the basic doctrines of salvation. "We hold unhesitatingly to the Bible teachings of the fall of man, the need of repentance, faith in Christ, regeneration, witness of the Spirit, Entire Sanctification by a gracious baptism with the Holy Ghost, Growth in Grace, and a constant life of righteousness."[1]

Since belief in the possibility of salvation for the sinner was almost universally held throughout Protestantism, it was not an area of contention in the ministry of Morrison. The same could not be said for his doctrine of "Entire Sanctification," hence it became one of the theological tenets for which he vigorously contended throughout the major portion of his ministry. Sample definitions of this doctrine from different periods of Morrison's life demonstrate the constancy of his teaching. "Christian perfection is purity of heart, it is perfection of love to God and His creatures, sin is all cleansed away; the character becomes stronger; wisdom increases; the heart is enlarged with love, and the soul grows in all the Christian graces."[2]

Nearly a quarter of a century later Morrison maintained that from the beginning the "Modern Holiness Movement" had insisted that

> there is a baptism with the Holy Ghost subsequent to a regeneration, that this baptism should be sought and may be received by all regenerated people, that the in-coming of the Spirit cleansing from the carnal mind, crucifies

> the sinful nature and that he then takes up his abode and keeps the temple in which he dwells to teach, guide and empower the children of God.³

"Man's sinful actions against God make him guilty," declared Morrison during the late years of his life, "and a subject for pardon. His depraved nature, which prompted his wicked actions, makes him a subject for cleansing. Sanctification is not a pardoning act; it is an act of purifying and cleansing."⁴

"The baptism with the Holy Ghost," according to Morrison, "is for believers only, and is never bestowed upon the unregenerated."⁵ In contending for this position it was pointed out that in the New Testament those present at Pentecost, Cornelius, and those converted in the revival in Samaria under the preaching of Philip, received the baptism with the Holy Spirit subsequent to their regeneration.

The object of this "second blessing," according to Morrison's teaching, was to deliver the Christian from the nature of sin, inherited by mankind as a result of the fall in Adam. "The most tremendous struggle of the human soul, is its struggle for freedom from its own downward bias and evil tendencies."⁶

> Any theory of Christian doctrine or teaching, that ignores or confutes the face of remaining sin, is unscriptural, out of harmony with the creeds of Christendom and contradicts the actual facts in Christian experience.⁷

Morrison made a clear distinction between the work of God in the "first work of grace," or regeneration, and in the "second work of grace," or entire sanctification. His doctrine rested upon the belief that "all human beings are naturally depraved, carnally minded, that man is fallen, that he has a corrupt and sinful nature."[8] This "sinful nature" was differentiated from acts of sin committed or "actual sin."

> The first blessing—regeneration—involves pardon for one's sins, and the cleansing away of the guilt which accrued because of sins committed. The soul receiving pardon stands justified, and being born again is adopted into the divine family—becomes a child of God. Entire sanctification involves the baptism with the Spirit, applying the cleansing blood and the purging out the natural depravity, the indwelling, or natural, sin, restoring the heart of the believer to the original state of purity, as God created it.[9]

As a further differentiation between the two works of grace, Morrison characterized the first as "the introduction of the new *life* into the soul," while "sanctification is the death of the old nature, and its eradication from the soul." The former is presented in Scripture, according to his view, "in the figure of birth, and the second in the figure of crucifixion or death."[10]

In order that there should be no confusion as to his position, Morrison made it clear that he did not agree with those who hold that "the carnal mind does not remain in those who have been regenerated, but that at regeneration the new life is imparted, and the old life is exterminated, and that no uncleanness remains in the heart of the regenerated."[11] On the other hand, he did agree with the Wesleyan teaching "that at regeneration a new life is imparted, and that at sanctification the remains of the old life is taken out of the heart."[12] In a similarly decisive manner Morrison made clear that the removal of the carnal nature was by divine act and not by a process of education or advancing culture.

This doctrine of entire sanctification had within it a positive as well as a negative element. Morrison held not only to the eradication of the carnal nature from the heart of the believer, but also to the filling of that heart with the divine love of God.

> As we have been taught and understand, entire sanctification not only embraces a gracious baptism with the Holy Ghost cleansing from all sin, but it also includes the shedding of the love of God abroad in the heart, and manifests itself in a most important and convincing way among one's fellow-beings.[13]

Morrison never believed in a limited atonement. He held that salvation was available to all men, from all sin, in this world- not in some manner made available only to a few, nor through the action of death.

> It is high time that the idea of a limited atonement be forever banished from the pulpit and driven out of the church. The whole tenor of the New Testament teaches that Jesus Christ by the grace of God, tasted death for every man, and that the blood of Jesus Christ cleanseth from all sin...the Scriptures teach that Jesus Christ came into the world and died to save men from *sin* and to save them in *this world*.[14]

As he believed that the initial work of salvation was for all and in this present life, so he taught that the second blessing was available for every believer who was willing to comply with the conditions requisite to its reception.

> The baptism with the Holy Ghost was for the eleven apostles, for the one hundred and nine persons in the upper room with them, for the three thousand, to be bestowed after they had received remission of sins, for the children of the three thousand, for *all* that are afar off, even as *many* as the Lord our God shall call. The word "call" here evidently means convert, or pardon, or regenerate. Even as many as God shall regenerate, have the promise of the baptism with the Holy Ghost.[15]

Although Morrison frequently spoke of this experience as "Christian Perfection," he did not imply that those attaining this grace had reached a spiritual condition beyond which further progress was impossible. Neither did he teach those possessing the experience were beyond temptation or the possibility of falling once more into "actual sin."

In advocating the doctrine of Entire Sanctification Morrison did not consider that he was propagating anything new. He firmly believed that his teaching was in harmony with that of early Methodism and of other religious leaders.

> Let it be remembered that the keynote of our message was Entire Sanctification as a second work of grace, cleansing the heart from inward sin. This had been a fundamental doctrine of original Methodism; in fact, more than any other doctrine it distinguished Methodism from other churches... This doctrine was regarded as so important by Mr. Wesley and the early preachers of the Methodist Church that no one

> was admitted as a minister into the conferences who was not wholly sanctified or believing in the doctrine, expecting to enter into the experience, and at the time of his admission groaning after it.[16]

While facing great opposition because of the doctrinal stand which he was taking in the columns of his paper, Morrison said: "I knew so well the foundations upon which I rested my faith, the Bible doctrine of Holiness and its interpretation by John and Charles Wesley, John Fletcher, Adam Clarke, Richard Watson, and others, that I had no trouble whatever on that score."[17]

There was no doctrine in Christian Theology for which Morrison fought more tenaciously than Entire Sanctification. He felt that if the church would stand firm on this issue many of its other problems would be solved, but failing here the door was opened to teachings which would ultimately bring ruin.

The rejection of the Holy Spirit was considered to be one of the greatest sins of the Church and was thought to be fatal to Christian experience.

> The greatest sin in the past history was the rejection of Jesus Christ by the church under the old dispensation. Often our minds have been amazed and our hearts have shuddered as we have read: "He came unto His own and His own received Him not." We have marveled at the stupidity and hardness of the Jews, who looked in the face of Jesus of Nazareth, heard his words, beheld His miracles, and yet ridiculed and rejected Him.

> Reader, think you that those ancient Jews were sinners above all men? I tell you they were not, and without doubt those members of the Christian Church under the new dispensation who reject the Holy Ghost, will commit even more grievous and fatal sin than that committed by the Jews in rejecting Christ. In proportion as our light is greater than was theirs, our sin will be more inexcusable than theirs. In the final day of judgment I would as soon stand there an ancient Jew who rejected Jesus, as to stand there a modem Gentile who rejected the Holy Ghost.[18]

Reaction to Modernism

The rise of modernism has been discussed in an earlier chapter and needs no reiteration. Morrison's reaction to this movement was indeed vociferous. His approach was not that of the scholar in answering argument for argument, but was more similar to the oratorical appeal of William Jennings Bryan. He wrote and preached in the spirit of those days of tumultuous theological conflict so characteristic of the early decades of the twentieth century.

In fairness to Morrison it should be said that while his reaction to modernism was violent, he was not a radical conservative whose prejudice made him blind to any benefits of the progressive movement. He felt that extremists in either direction were limiting their usefulness.

> There is no doubt we have some preachers who are too conservative; they are backing into the future; they are too quiet and easy; they fail to arouse the people, awaken the mind, stir the conscience, provoke thought, agitate and move

things forward. Such men are an incubus; they hinder the work of the Lord; they encumber the church; they occupy places and consume time that might be used to gracious advantage by men who would do something. We have others who boast that they are progressives; they are constantly seeking to supplant the old doctrines and old methods with something *new*.[19]

We are in danger that conservatism go to sleep upon the bed of satisfaction and ease and let opportunities pass by unimproved. There are some conservatives who will patiently plow and cultivate last year's corn-stalks with a sort of hope that they will be able to gather from them another harvest of roasting ears...The progressive is just as unwise and more dangerous who will layoff his coat, seize an axe with enthusiasm and chop down a good apple tree that has borne fruit for many years and is full of promise for the future simply because it is old. The matter of great importance is that we shall learn to distinguish between last year's corn-stalks and old orchards in good bearing.[20]

From Morrison's writings during the period of the 1920's, it appears that his most constant characterization of the modernists was that they had a negative approach with many statements as to what they did not believe, but with little or no constructive program for the rescue of a fallen race.

True, the modernists are as yet up in the air; they have some hesitation as to where they shall light, and with whom they shall settle down for permanent abode and active service.

> As yet, they have no inspired Bible, no divine atoning Christ, able to save from sin, no system of theology, no fixed creed, no hymnology, no enthusiastic evangelism to win sinners from the ruin of their wickedness to a Savior. The fact is, there is a question in their minds as to whether there is any real sin, or the need of a Savior.[21]

Because of what Morrison felt the Modernists believed and did not believe—because of their efforts to destroy the very foundations upon which American Christianity had been founded- they should be opposed with deadly earnestness, but without anger.

> The time has come to send this bedlam of ecclesiastical skeptics to the rear. They are incompetent for leadership; they give an uncertain sound. To accept their illogical, theological crazy-quilt of patchwork would be to confess that we have followed a will-o-the-wisp of falsehood; it would be to tear down the beautiful structure of our holy sanctuary and to lock the wheels of modern progress; to turn out the lights of divine truth and become the followers of conceited blind leaders who would land us in the ditch of unbelief, evolution, bloodshed, and ruin...[22]

Morrison's reaction to the "Modernist-Fundamentalist" controversy was seen not only in his vociferous attack upon all shades of "modernism" and "liberalism," but was also reflected in his advocacy of other phases of theology such as his Bibliology, Christology, and Eschatology.

Bibliology

H. C. Morrison believed all of the Bible, and believed that it was infallibly inspired revelation of God which was fundamental to the whole structure of Christian faith and doctrine. "The Bible," he said, "is the foundation upon which the whole superstructure of our Christianity rests. We cannot possibly destroy the foundation and preserve the superstructure intact."[23] He held that Christ as the Son of God and

> only Savior of mankind, nowhere undertook to separate himself from the Holy Scriptures. Always, and everywhere, he quoted the Scriptures, called on his enemies to search the Scriptures, and declared that the word of God should not pass away; based his identity, and proved his sonship out of the Scriptures, and challenged men to go to the Scriptures for the proof of all he claimed for himself.[24]

He firmly declared that "a Bible held up to ridicule, closed up and put aside, is not going to save anyone. It must be read, preached, defended, inculcated, believed and practiced in order that it may become efficacious in the salvation of men."[25] He did not contend, however, that the mere writing of the Scriptures made them infallible truth, but rather that "it is eternal truth, or it never would have been written."[26]

The higher-critics of Morrison's day attacked the authenticity of much of the Old Testament. The attack was especially concentrated on the Mosaic authorship of the Pentateuch. Morrison affirmed his faith in the inspiration of the Old Testament, and pointed to the discoveries of archaeology as one of the bases upon which he rested his credence in the

Mosaic authorship of the first five books. Although early critics had maintained that in Moses' time methods of writing were unknown, Morrison pointed out that archaeologists had shown that there was considerable literature during that period. A comparison of the contemporary writings with the higher level of literature of the first five books of the Holy Scriptures has, he said, made it easy for Christians "to attribute them to the pen of an inspired man who wrote down for his fellow-beings of all time to come, the fundamental law that ought to govern and guide in all the realms of human intercourse and society."[27]

Morrison's outstanding proof, was the use which Jesus made of not only the Pentateuch, but also all the Old Testament Scriptures: "The many quotations of our Lord Jesus, from the Old Testament Scriptures show clearly that He placed His endorsement fully upon those writings, and those who really accept Jesus Christ as the Messiah, must accept the old books of the Bible, as inspired, and of divine origin and authority."[28]

Morrison proclaimed his acceptance of the miracles of the Bible in as ardent a manner as the "destructive critics" denied them:

> This question is frequently asked me, Do you believe in miracles? I certainly do. I believe the Bible. I believe in the record of miracles in Old Testament and New as accurate and truthful. No one can believe the New Testament and not believe in miracles. Take the Gospel of Mark, for instance; I think more than half of the verses of this gospel is a record of miracles. Suppose you take your scissors and cut out all that Mark says about miracles, what would you have left? If you cannot believe what Mark says about these wonderful healings performed by our Lord, by what sort of mental process are you

> going to believe what he says of the teachings and doings of our Lord?
>
> I do not believe in the men who do not believe in miracles. I cannot understand how any man can claim that the miracles recorded in the gospels are forgeries, and the other parts of the gospel inspired and trustworthy.

It was not Morrison's position that all critical study of the Bible was destructive, but he did oppose those who were constantly trying to cast doubt on the authority of the Bible and implying that it *contained* the word of God rather than *being* in its entirety the word of God.

> Those skeptical preachers who assume to be devoutly religious, and eager for the uplift of society and the development of the spiritual life of the masses, and yet question the inspiration of the Scriptures, will tell you that the Bible *contains* the word of God, but they are never positive with reference to what part of it is the word of God.[29]

Morrison did not concur with those who held that one "need not be uneasy about the Bible. If it is inspired it will take care of itself. It cannot be destroyed."[30] He believed, rather, that the Bible must be not only defended but also preached. It was through the preaching of the whole Bible, not just one theme such as entire sanctification, that the spiritual redemption and social uplift of the world would be attained. As a result of the intensity of his convictions on this subject he wrote many articles in opposition to those who disapproved the doctrine of the divine inspiration of the Scriptures.

In 1927 an article was published in *The Pentecostal Herald*—a paragraph from which seems a fitting summary of Morrison's bibliology:

> Aside from the fact that the Bible is an inspired Book, revealing the laws of God for the just, equal and happy regulation of society, and the Gospel plans for the saving of a lost race, it is also the most interesting Book in all the world's literature. Its records are the most ancient; its histories the most accurate; its incidents the most thrilling to be found anywhere on the printed page. Where will one find such startling stories of war, such peaceful pastoral tales, such heartwarming romances of love as are found related in the sacred pages of the Bibles? Its poetry is pitched on the highest plane, its proverbs contains the richest wisdom, its prophecies reveal the future and its promises give anchorage and hope to the soul. The whole of it leads one to bow at the feet of the Lord Jesus Christ, trust in him as a Savior, and worship him as a God.[31]

Christology

Although the Doctrine of Christ was not the center of controversy as were the subjects discussed above, still there were enough facets of the theory under debate to warrant a presentation of Morrison's views. During a period when S. J. Case, of the University of Chicago, and the men of his school of thought were placing emphasis upon the "historic Jesus," Morrison emphasized the attribute of eternity in Christ by saying: "I believe in Jesus Christ, that he existed before all things and all men; that by the power of the Holy Ghost he was incarnated; that in this sense he was the only begotten Son of God…"

One of the most involved phases of Morrison's Christological creed was the doctrine of the Incarnation of Christ, or the union of the pre-existent Son of God with humanity. This included the dogma of the virgin birth of Jesus, to which Morrison gave wholehearted assent.

> It must not be forgotten that the annunciation angel appeared unto Mary and announced to her that the Holy Spirit should generate within her a child who was to be born, and named Jesus, because he was to be a redeemer, that is, to take away the sins of the people. Man had nothing to do with the generation of our Lord. Joseph, to be sure, had visitations from an angel, but it was only to reveal to him the fact that his wife was virtuous and true, and that the child to be born of her was created by the Holy Spirit.[32]

It was through this miraculous entrance of Jesus into the world, Morrison declared, that Christ was kept from the fallen and sinful nature which had been inherited by all of Adam's race.

If one holds to the Incarnation of Christ it follows naturally to believe in the deity of Jesus. This seemed to create no problem for Morrison as he held that Christ was the Messiah whose coming was prophesied throughout the Old Testament, and that he was virgin born. The affirmations of Morrison's acceptance of the deity of Jesus were many, but to him one of the greatest proofs of the fact was the attestation of the Sonship of Jesus given by God at the time of Jesus' baptism, and again on the Mount of Transfiguration. It was difficult for Morrison to accept as real friends of God those who did not adhere to this principle: "...it is useless to talk to us about the beautiful lives, the splendid courage of the Scriptures, question the Deity of Jesus, and ridicule the doctrine of the new birth. Such men are enemies of God..."[33]

The humanity of Christ was considered to be as important a factor, though perhaps not quite so controversial.

> We can no more permit the theologian and philosopher to rob us of the humanity of Jesus, than we can permit the destructive critic and skeptic to rob us of the deity of Jesus. We must keep in our thought, worship in our heart, and proclaim in our message to the people the Christ of the gospels, that human-divine being, who lived, walked and talked with the disciples; that human Christ who can be touched with the feeling of our infirmities; that divine Christ who is able to save to the uttermost, who is the same yesterday, today and forever.[34]

The dual nature of the Incarnate Christ was illustrated in one of Morrison's sermons by means of a series of contrasts:

> As we follow Him there is no doubt that He is God manifest in the flesh. He walks like a man, but He works like a God. We behold His humanity when He lay sleeping in the boat, and His deity when He arises and rebukes the wind and storm, and the tempest sinks into silence at His command. He weeps like a man at Lazarus' tomb, but with god-like voice He breaks the power of death and brings him forth alive. As a man, He sits hungry at the well's mouth; like a

> God, He breaks the few loaves and little fishes and feeds the multitude. Like a man, He goes into the mountains for prayer; like a God He walks the waves of the sea of Galilee and overtakes His disciples who have gone forth in the ship. Like a man, He climbs the mountain; transfigured like a God he stands upon its crest in garments whiter than the light.
>
> What a marvelous combination of the two natures- human and divine! Spirit begotten and virgin born...[35]

The incarnation was a necessary part of God's plan of redemption, for by it a mediator between God and man was provided. "Man's condition," said Morrison, "was such that it was necessary to offer him a Redeemer so human that he could sympathize with him, and so divine that He could save him."[36] The incarnation revealed man to God in an experiential manner never before known by Him; and at the same time the Incarnate Christ became such a full and complete revelation of God to man that Jesus could say, "He that hath seen me hath seen the Father."[37]

A final point of contention concerning the person of Christ has centered around the account of his resurrection from death. Morrison left no doubt as to his faith in the literal, bodily resurrection of Jesus.

> Before His crucifixion He told them plainly that He would die. At least one of them saw Him die, and no doubt assisted in His burial. They saw His empty tomb; they looked into His face after He arose; they heard and recognized His voice; they beheld the nail-prints inflicted by His

crucifiers. They identified Him absolutely, and worshipped their risen Lord with inexpressible love and joy. They bore witness to the world with tongue and pen, to His life, teachings, death, resurrection—His eternal Sonship—His power to forgive sins, and His ascension into glory. Their writings have stood the test of the ages; they are the comfort and hope of the world.[38]

"The resurrection of our Lord Jesus Christ," Morrison declared, "is, to all believers, the final and satisfactory proof of his Godhead. The prophecies he uttered and the miracles he performed were convincing proof that he was a teacher come from God, but his resurrection from the death was the positive proof that he was God manifest in the flesh."[39] So important did Morrison consider the acceptance of this tenet that he doubted whether one who rejected it was a true Christian: "It is safe to say that no one can be, in a true sense, a disciple of the Lord Jesus, and saved from sin through the merit of his death, who does not fully, unwaveringly believe in his resurrection."[40]

Eschatology

Morrison was not a fanatic in his study of the prophets and in his advocacy of the pre-millennial coming of Christ for the doctrines discussed above were, to him, pre-eminent. He did, however, write voluminously on eschatology in *The Pentecostal Herald* and in separately published books. Concerning the value of prophetic study he said: "...we believe a thoughtful study of prophecy is not only a mental stimulus, but most informing with regard to what the future holds, and a gracious means of grace; it also gives a consciousness of being taken into confidence with the Lord."[41] "The great pivotal events of the history of the world are so faithfully foretold and so accurately described by ancient prophets, that there is but one possible way to account for their knowledge of coming events, and this is, they were inspired by the Holy Spirit."[42] He felt that the fulfillment of prophecy was one of the effective proofs of the existence of God.

Of great interest to Morrison were the prophecies relative to the return of the Jews to Palestine. He thought that the freeing of Palestine from Turkish control during World War One and the consequent return of the Jews to that country under the auspices of the Zionist Movement, were all in harmony with Biblical prophecy.

Of greater theological importance than the return of the Jews was Morrison's interest in the second coming of Jesus. On one occasion he gave a careful summary of the views held by two of the schools of thought relative to the return of Christ to this earth:

> Post-millennialists believe the preaching of the gospel will so powerfully influence society that gradually the world will be converted, evil will be overcome, and the millennium—a thousand years of universal peace and blessedness—will come upon the earth; and that at the end of this thousand years the Lord Jesus Christ will appear in great glory and power to inaugurate the judgment, catch away His bride into heaven, and drive the wicked into outer darkness.

> Pre-millennialists believe that the gospel must be preached to all the world for a witness, that by many it will be rejected, that wicked men will wax worse and worse; that Christ's coming will be as in the days of Noah, when the world is not expecting or desiring Him; and while vast

> multitudes are living in rebellion and sin, that just as Noah gathered the few righteous persons into the ark, so the Lord Jesus will gather His redeemed bride into the place prepared for them, and then, as the flood destroyed the wicked in the days of Noah, so great tribulation will come upon the earth; that later on Jesus will appear with His people, set up His Kingdom, bind and cast Satan into the pit and reign in great glory for a thousand years.[43]

Morrison rejected the former view and gave wholehearted assent to the latter.

It was Morrison's conviction that upon the bodily return of Christ to earth He would set up a temporal kingdom. Christ, as king, would rule the entire world for a period of a thousand years. During this period, Satan having been bound, peace and happiness would be found everywhere. The saints of previous ages would be raised from the dead in order that they might assist Christ in his millennial government.[44]

The last great eschatological event in Morrison's opinion would be the final judgment. Immediately following the millennial reign, Satan would be released for a short period of apostasy at the conclusion of which all men from all ages would be gathered before the throne of God for final judgment of all deeds done in the flesh. The righteous should there be rewarded with everlasting life in heaven, while the unrepentant sinners would suffer everlasting punishment in the torments of hell.

Social Teachings

Morrison's energies were not entirely concentrated on the purely theological issues of his day, for his interests included a wide variety of social problems. Their relative importance was such as to merit only brief attention, but to present the life and work of H. C. Morrison without mentioning his views on such subjects as the prohibition movement, movies, dancing, tobacco, politics and Negro education would be unfair.

From the early years of his ministry, Morrison was a bitter opponent of the liquor traffic. He supported the prohibition movement in its drive for the adoption of the eighteenth amendment. In 1928 he opposed the candidacy of "Al" Smith for the presidency because of his stand on the liquor question, and in 1933 he grieved over F. D. Roosevelt's signing of the "Beer bill." His characterization in 1928 of the liquor traffic is illustrative of his attitude:

> The highway robber puts his pistol to your head and takes your money, but the liquor traffic puts its bottle to your mouth, takes your money, addles your brain, breaks down your health, destroys your body, and damns your soul. The liquor traffic is utterly and absolutely of the devil. It ought to be driven off the earth and out of the world. The friends, aiders, and abettors of the liquor traffic are the enemies of God and humanity.[45]

As the movie industry began to flourish during the second decade of the twentieth century many churches turned to the use of moving pictures as a substitute for the Sunday evening evangelistic sermon. Morrison opposed such action with all the ardor at his command and did not relent throughout the remainder of his life:

> We must rally every possible spiritual force against this whole movie business which

> proposes to offer itself as a substitute for the gospel, divert our attention from the Holy Ghost, and blast the Church with worldliness.[46]

During the 1920's there was a great deal of agitation in the Methodist Episcopal Church, South, for the removal of the disciplinary rule against dancing. This stimulated Morrison to an attack on the social dance as an evil which should, if possible, be eliminated: "The dance craze is on with full blast... Every disciple of Jesus Christ must unsheathe his or her sword against this dancing assault upon decency and fight against it with unrelenting energy."[47]

Early in Morrison's ministry he quit using tobacco and from that time on he opposed its use by anyone, but especially ministers. The intensity of his feeling can be seen through a paragraph taken from one of his books:

> The filthy tobacco habit must be swept from our pulpits. It is a shame that a minister of the gospel of freedom in Christ should stand up to proclaim his message, reeking with the stains and stench of tobacco. The conflict against this selfish, unhealthy, expensive habit only excusable in the untaught heathen, may be long and hard, but victory is sure to come.[48]

Morrison joined with other ministers of similar views, and in 1901 they passed a resolution in the Kentucky Annual Conference memorializing the General Conference to place a paragraph in the *Discipline* discouraging the use of tobacco by ministers and laymen.[49] Although no affirmative action was taken by the General Conference at that time, Morrison and his friends continued their fight until some years later legislation was passed prohibiting the use of tobacco by young ministers who were being received into the conference.[50] In 1926, as a member of the General Conference, he refused to "vote to elect any man to the bishopric who uses tobacco."[51] As late as 1938, he wrote: "It's a strange thing that our American people should have fallen into a habit so expensive, so useless, so unkindly, and unhealthy as that of smoking [and] chewing this filthy weed."[52]

Contrary to the view held by many that religion and politics do not mix, Morrison believed: "If a man's religion does not affect his politics he ought to throw it away and seek the religion of the Lord Jesus Christ. That will affect his entire life, his thoughts, desires, and actions. To be a true Christian man is to vote as one prays."[53] That he not only had views, but that he also expressed them can be demonstrated with a few illustrations.

Although normally a Democrat, Morrison felt from the first that Franklin D. Roosevelt was backed by Tammany Hall, and he never approved of the Roosevelt administration. In 1936 he said, "I doubt if in the history of this nation there has been a more Godless administration in Washington City than at the present time. The White House is anything but an example for the family life of the nation."[54] It was during those years, and perhaps as a result of the Roosevelt administration, that Morrison advocated a constitutional amendment providing for the election of the President of the United States for a six-year term without possibility of reelection.[55] He considered the recognition of Russia by the Roosevelt regime a "serious mistake."[56]

During the depression years of the 1930's, Morrison wrote many articles concerning the economic situation. He blamed the great industrial organizations, chain stores, and the extensive use of modern machinery (especially the automobile) for creating the deplorable financial situation. His philosophy of recovery seemed to have been a return to the "good old days" when fire-wood was traded for shoes, and horses ate oats instead of automobiles burning gasoline. He saw the loss of some old farm markets, but he seemed to fail to see the new source of income which had been created by industrialization.

A phase of the race problem, always a touchy one in America, shall serve as a final illustration of Morrison's views on social questions. In 1906 he expressed an opinion that society would be benefited by the education of the Negro. He suggested that the Negro was capable of being educated and that he would become a better citizen as a result of training:

> The educated [Negroes] have more self respect, are more industrious, and use the proceeds of their labor to best advantage, buy property, build and furnish homes, and become a factor in the general building up of society, and the wealth and welfare of the country. The most horrible crimes committed in recent years in the South by Negro men, have in not one instance been committed by men educated in the training schools for colored people, but in every instance by the most ignorant and brutal.[57]

H. C. Morrison was neither a scholar nor a theologian, but he was a Christian general directing his forces in a great crusade supporting all that he felt to be righteous, and attacking whatever appeared to him as being sinful and unholy. With unflinching courage he stood for the right as he saw the right. Though not a theologian his theological emphasis have been deeply impressed upon the thinking of the modern holiness movement.

Notes

[1] *The Pentecostal Herald.*

[2] H. C. Morrison, *Life Sketches and Sermons* (Louisville, 1903). Hereafter referred to as *Life Sketches and Sermons.*

[3] *The Pentecostal Herald.*

[4] *Ibid.*

[5] "The Revival of the Camp Meeting by the Holiness Groups."

[6] *Open Letters to the Bishops.*

[7] *Ibid.*

[8] *The Pentecostal Herald.*

[9] *Ibid.*

[10] *Life Sketches and Sermons.*

[11] *The Pentecostal Herald.*

[12] *Ibid.*

[13] *Ibid.*

[14] *Ibid.*

[15] H. C. Morrison, *The World War in Prophecy* (Louisville, 1900). Hereafter referred to as *The World War in Prophecy.* Digital copy freely available from First Fruits Press: <http://place.asburyseminary.edu/firstfruitsheritagematerial/28/>

[16] *The Pentecostal Herald.*

[17] *Ibid.*

[18] *The World War in Prophecy.*

[19] *The Pentecostal Herald.*

[20] *Ibid.*

[21] *Ibid.*

[22] *Ibid.*

[23] *Ibid.*

[24] *Ibid.*

[25] *Open Letters to the Bishops.*

[26] *The Pentecostal Herald.*

[27] *Ibid.*

[28] *Ibid.*

[29] *Ibid.*

[30] *Ibid.*

[31] *Ibid.*

[32] *Ibid.*

[33] *Ibid.*

[34] H. C. Morrison, *Commencement Sermons Delivered in Asbury College Chapel* (Louisville, 1915). Digital copy freely available from First Fruits Press:
<http://place.asburyseminary.edu/firstfruitsheritagematerial/25/>

[35] *Ibid.*

[36] *Ibid.*

[37] *Ibid.*

[38] *The Pentecostal Herald.*

[39] *Ibid.*

[40] *Ibid.*

[41] *Ibid.*

[42] H. C. Morrison, *The World War in Prophecy* (Louisville, 1917).

[43] H. C. Morrison, *The Second Coming of Christ* (Louisville, 1934). Digital copy freely available from First Fruits Press: <http://place.asburyseminary.edu/firstfruitsheritagematerial/27/>

[44] H. C. Morrison, *Will God Set Up a Visible Kingdom on Earth* (Louisville, 1934). Digital copy freely available from First Fruits Press: <http://place.asburyseminary.edu/firstfruitsheritagematerial/21/>

[45] *The Pentecostal Herald.*

[46] *Ibid.*

[47] *Ibid.*

[48] *Open Letters to the Bishops.*

[49] "Conference Minutes."

[50] *The Doctrines and Discipline of the Methodist Episcopal Church*

[51] *The Pentecostal Herald.*

[52] *Ibid.*

[53] *Ibid.*

[54] H. C. Morrison, "Diary," 1893, 1895-1910; 1913-41.

[55] *The Pentecostal Herald.*

[56] *Ibid.*

[57] *Ibid.*

Chapter 14
An Influential Life

A summary of major achievements throughout the life of Henry Clay Morrison seems a suitable theme for the concluding chapter. To review the accomplishments of the man and to present the testimonials of persons who worked and associated with him would seem appropriate. If such an analysis marshals evidence of Morrison's influence having been both widespread and of such permanent nature as to warrant the inclusion of his name among the influential religious leaders in American history, then one of the questions which stimulated this study shall have been answered.

Although the method of approach is largely a resume of those accomplishments which contributed to his moral and spiritual influence, it should be remembered that Morrison was a man with faults as well as virtues. It was well known that he loved positions of leadership; that he was moody and made "snap" judgments, that he was quick to interrupt and correct others who were speaking before him—something he would not have appreciated had it been practiced on him; and that it was difficult for him to acknowledge a mistake and openly apologize. But an expression made after Morrison's death by a man who was for years a friend and co-worker with Morrison demonstrates a considered judgment of both his faults and virtues.

> His [Morrison's] gifts have been so often and well extolled, and worthily so, that we may give the impression that he was more than mortal. But let us not forget that he was human and had imperfections, many of them. Yet while we acknowledge this in the personality of this extraordinary man it may be softened by an expression from Goldsmith's *Village Minister*, "E'en his failings leaned to virtue's side." He once told a friend of mine, "Brasher is moody," – the quality he himself possessed in such a marked degree…When one brother in the ministry fell, he wrote him that he feared his lust for leadership had been the cause of his fall. The fallen brother wrote back saying that was the quality he had always thought was Brother Morrison's.
>
> ....
>
> No. We will keep him human, but glorify God for the tremendous influence of his life and the achievements of some sixty-five years of ministry and administrative labors. Without grace he would have been a dangerous man with whom to interfere.[1]

Influence as Editor, Author, and Publisher

Morrison was one of the most influential among the editors of independent holiness papers. For fifty-three years he continued as active editor of his periodical. It has been said that few if any other men in America have continued in active editorial work on a religious paper for so long a time.[2] Morrison estimated that at the beginning of the paper's fortieth year he had written enough editorial material to have filled "one hundred volumes of two hundred pages each, with much matter to spare."[3] The editorial writings of fourteen years were added before his pen was laid down the last time.

The wide distribution of *The Pentecostal Herald* indicates something of its influence. During the fifty three years of his editorship nearly sixty-five million copies were distributed. The circulation grew from the insignificant 500 copies of the first issue in 1888 to a weekly circulation of 55,000 during the summer of 1942. The average weekly circulation for the latter half of that period was thirty thousand. As an example of the geographic area covered, in 1945 *The Herald* was mailed to at least forty-six states, the District of Columbia, and 566 copies were sent to foreign countries.

Throughout the years the expressions of appreciation for spiritual help received through the reading of *The Pentecostal Herald* have been legion. J. W. Weldon, President of the Louisville Conference Historical Society, in an address given at the Sesquicentennial Celebration of Kentucky Methodism, appraised *The Herald* as follows:

> As an independent religious periodical, it has enjoyed a large circulation both with reference to its subscribers and the geographical area covered. I seriously doubt if there is another man in world-wide Methodism whose messages, week by week, reach more people and whose influence in promoting experimental religion is as great today as that of Dr. H. C. Morrison...[4]

The Pentecostal Herald has been the financial lifeline of both Asbury College and Asbury Theological Seminary. Appeals to its 30,000 subscribers supplied a major source of income for the college during the thirty years of Morrison's association with them.[5] In 1939, during the campaign to payoff the indebtedness of the college, Morrison said, "I am confident that eighty-five or ninety percent of the money that has gone into Asbury College has come from readers of *The Herald*..."[6] When the Seminary was first organized it relied largely for financial support upon contributions sent as a result of appeals made by Morrison in the columns of this paper. Even today, a substantial portion of its total income is received as a direct result of the influence of *The Herald*.

Besides being an editor, Morrison was a popular author, having written at least twenty-five books. Several of these sold as many as seventy thousand copies. One went through eight editions in six months and another, after having been translated into both the Japanese and Chinese languages, had a large sale in the Orient as well as in America. James W. Hervey's reaction to Morrison's writings was no doubt characteristic of many readers:

> I read everything that Dr. Morrison writes. His books of sermons are models of spiritual power. His editorials in *The Herald* constitute a standard of spiritual life and doctrine, which Methodism would do well to stand by. I have the portrait of this mighty preacher on the wall of my study as an inspiration to my eye, and I read his paper and books to cause my heart to burn with zeal for the gospel.[7]

The organization and subsequent enlargement of the Pentecostal Publishing Company should be mentioned as an achievement of Morrison. From his first venture in 1888 as an editor and publisher, when he was left with a deficit of fifty cents after the first issue of *The Old Methodist,* he developed his business into the Pentecostal Publishing Company. Since

Morrison's death in 1942, it has been listed as an asset of three hundred thousand dollars toward the endowment of Asbury Theological Seminary. During a period of fifty years the Pentecostal Publishing Company has printed approximately five million books and pamphlets. For more than a decade it has sold, through its bookstore in Louisville, Kentucky, an average of more than fifty thousand dollars worth of Bibles each year, thus making it one of the twelve largest retail distributors of Bibles in America. To be sure, this achievement has not been the result of Morrison's effort alone, but without him there would have been no such organization.

Influence as an Educational Administrator

Without Morrison there would be no Asbury College or Asbury Theological Seminary today. He had a constant interest in the college from its organization in 1890. From 1907-1942, he was a member of its Board of Trustees, and for twenty-three years of that time served as president of that body.[8] Morrison served the school as its president on two occasions, 1910-1925, and again from September 1933 until June 1940—a total of twenty-two years. Both terms as president were terminated by his voluntary resignation. In 1923 he founded Asbury Theological Seminary and continued as its president until his death in 1942. It is not necessary to reiterate the struggles or the successes in either the financial or academic areas of these two schools. It is sufficient to say that Morrison was so closely associated with both of them that a large share of the credit for their accomplishments must be given to him.

All of the administrative achievements previously recounted might be freely acknowledged and still the question of Morrison's real influence as an educational leader could remain unanswered. His contribution to society as an educational leader cannot be properly evaluated until it is considered in the light of the benefits accruing through the life and work of students who have gone from the halls of Asbury College.

The potential influence of this school can be partially measured by the number of students enrolled and by the geographical areas into which they went. From a total enrollment of 212 during his first year, 1910-1911, the number was increased to 556 *bona fide* college students in 1924-1925, the last year of Morrison's first term as president. Besides the average number of registrants in the college during Morrison's affiliation as administrator, registration records show that students had come from forty-seven states and eighteen foreign countries. So widespread was the geographic distribution that, according to a study made by Professor C. R. Foster of Rutgers University and Paul S. Dwyer of Antioch College, Asbury was rated the second most national college in America. Morrison was given credit for this geographic spread within the student body.

Throughout the years the contributions of Asbury College as a center of Christian education have been sufficiently great to create its reputation as having sent out as many, or more, Christian workers than any liberal arts college in America.

> Asbury College is known all over the world for having trained more preachers and missionaries than any other Liberal Arts College in America during the past 50 years; for sending more chaplains into the Armed Services than any other college during the last war; and for being one of the most cosmopolitan colleges in America.[9]

The influence of Asbury College as a training center for Christian workers has been demonstrated in the missionary interest of many of its graduates. One newspaper reporter accredited Asbury College with having furnished "more foreign missionaries than any other school in America, irrespective of size..."[10] The school has been equally well-known for its preparation of young men for the ministry, especially of the Methodist Church. By 1930, at least 130 preachers, formerly Asbury students, were active in the ministry of Kentucky Methodism. Two years later a member of the Kentucky Conference appraised its personnel.

> The soul winners of our Conference are holiness men. Most of the additions to the membership for several years have been educated in Asbury College which is strictly a holiness school. At the present time a majority of our members were educated in that college and are professors of sanctification... With such an equipment our Conference ought to grow in grace and in numbers.[11]

As an illustration of some outstanding alumni of Asbury College and the responsible positions which they have held a few names have been selected from among the many that might be listed:

- Donald E. Wilson, writer and author, of Pasadena, California
- Eugene A. Erny, for many years President of the Oriental Missionary Society, Los Angeles
- John O. Gross, who served as Executive Secretary of the General Board of Education of the Methodist Church, Nashville, Tennessee
- John H. Furbay, Director of TWA Global Air World Education, New York City

- W. G. Cram, for many years General Secretary of the Board of Missions of the Methodist Episcopal Church, South
- Chester A. McPheeters, pastor of the Metropolitan Methodist Church, Detroit, Michigan
- Edward L. R. Elson, minister of the National Presbyterian Church, Washington, D. C.
- Bishops J. Wascom Pickett, and Fred B. Fisher of India
- E. Stanley Jones, world missionary and churchman in India
- C. Kildow Lovejoy, president and general manager of the Kildow Hotels, Lexington, Kentucky
- S. E. McCreeless, president of the American Hospital and Life Insurance Company, San Antonio, Texas.

Tributes paid by some of these men to the influence of Asbury College upon their lives indicate something of the value to society of the school which was kept from failure in 1910 and again in 1933 by H. C. Morrison. Lovejoy said: "I am grateful for the privilege of speaking a word for my Christ and to tell what Asbury College has meant to me down through the years. I have taken God as my partner in all my business affairs, and the joy of His blessings in immeasurable."[12] S. E. McCreeless stated, "as a business executive with tremendous personnel and public relations responsibilities, every contribution Asbury made to me has been of value in my business, social, and church life."[13] On another occasion he wrote: "It has been my privilege to know many fine people through the years but I consider the privilege of having known Dr. Morrison as intimately and well as I did one of the greatest privileges of my career."[14]

Bishop Fisher spoke earnestly of the influence of Asbury College upon his life:

> It is an easy task...for me to recall the profound impression made upon my life and thought by Asbury College. It was here that my personal religious experience took such form and found such expression as to make doubt impossible during all the succeeding years...It was here that I caught for the first time that vision of the 'world's need which it seemed to me Christ must have had...My missionary vision came to me at Asbury.[15]

Dr. Edward L. R. Elson, minister of the National Presbyterian Church in Washington, D. C.—the church home of former President and Mrs. Dwight D. Eisenhower—recently wrote concerning Asbury College:

> My Alma Mater not only provided for me an adequate academic training but the classroom, laboratory, library, dormitory, athletic field and social halls were so infused with the Christian spirit as to permanently contribute to the development of Christian character. At Asbury College, I developed those principles of spiritual disciplines of Bible study, meditation and prayer which have been the foundation of my life throughout all the years of my life, and for which I shall be eternally thankful.[16]

In an evaluation of the educational influence of Morrison, his part in the founding and carrying on of Asbury Theological Seminary should not be overlooked. Founded in 1923, it continued under the personal direction of Morrison until his death in 1942. Until 1945 it was the only graduate theological school in America placing strong emphasis upon the Wesleyan doctrine of entire sanctification as a second work of grace, subsequent to regeneration. The enrollment showed a steady increase from three the first year, 1923-1924, to eighty-nine in 1941-1942. Since that time it has continued to grow until in 1948 it was ranked as the tenth largest *bona fide* graduate theological school in America.[17] At the close of the commencement program in 1942, a total of 226 persons had been granted the B. D. degree by Asbury Theological Seminary. That the influence of the institution founded by Morrison has continued after his death can be seen through statistics which show that by June 1953 a total of 836 degrees had been granted, and a total of 2,143 different individuals had matriculated in Asbury Theological Seminary by the close of the spring quarter, 1954.

Contrary to the usual expectation, Morrison as an administrator exerted a personal influence not only upon the organization but also in the lives of the students, which may be seen through the many testimonials which have been given. A few quotations taken from returns received in response to the "Asbury Alumni Questionnaire on Henry Clay Morrison," illustrate this point.

> Dr. Morrison's ministry in Asbury and his work as President of Asbury had a great influence on my life. The principles he taught have been instilled in my life. He moved with authority and was respected and liked by all the students.[18]
>
> Dr. Morrison's devotion to his calling and to Jesus Christ his Lord, his poise and strength of character, his courage and convictions, along with his personal interest in me had a profound influence over me and largely made me what I am today.[19]

> I believe he influenced my life more than any other man—he left his stamp deep in my life—I answered the call to preach while in my early years attending Asbury College while he was president.
>
> I have a picture of Dr. Morrison in my study. I suppose I love and appreciate him more than any man I ever met except my father. I never get away from his influence.[20]
>
> By his superb preaching he led me to a deeper love for Christ and lofty appreciation of the Gospel of the New Covenant, and of the efficacy of inspired pulpit oratory.[21]
>
> I was always impressed by the dynamic and forcefulness of his strong, vigorous personality. I appreciated his positiveness. There was no compromise in him. This appealed to me and made me determined to be like that.[22]

The two educational institutions, Asbury College, and Asbury Theological Seminary, stand as monuments to the work of H. C. Morrison. The hundreds of graduates who have gone out, and will be going out, from the halls of these two schools, serve as living testimonials to Morrison's influence as an educator.

Influence as a Preacher

H. C. Morrison was pre-eminently a preacher. No matter how much he may have enjoyed the other phases of Christian activity, he was happiest when from behind the sacred desk he was able to proclaim the Gospel of the unsearchable riches of Christ. As one friend said, "Great as were his many qualities, his power in the pulpit and public address was his greatest."[23] From the time he received his first license to preach in the summer of 1878, there was not a year in which he was not actively engaged in preaching. At the close of sixty-three and a half years in the ministry, death took him while he was in the midst of a revival campaign.

Morrison loved to preach. He not only enjoyed the ministry, but the records show that he was a successful preacher. From a humble beginning as assistant preacher on the Floydsburg Circuit, Morrison rose to the leadership of the Methodist Church in Frankfort, one of the best appointments in the Kentucky Conference. Opportunities to serve as pastor of still larger churches in other Conferences were offered to him.

In 1890, Morrison "located" from his Conference and for the next fifty-one and a half years gave as much of his time to evangelism as his other responsibilities and his physical strength would permit. Throughout those years he conducted evangelistic campaigns in at least forty states, and thirteen other countries. In America, Morrison's meetings included the large churches as well as the small ones. His itinerary included practically all of the large cities in the United States. As a summary it has been estimated that Morrison held at least "1200 revivals, preached not less than 15,000 times, traveled over 500,000 miles and saw more than 30,000 people converted at his altars" during the sixty-three years of ministry.[24]

Throughout most of Morrison's half century of evangelism he was also a well known camp meeting preacher. He preached in approximately 250 such campaigns. Since this program occupied his time for nearly three months every summer he considered that about one-fourth of each year, or a total of nearly twelve years, was spent in camp meeting work. To anyone who is familiar with the history of the holiness camp meeting, as it flourished during the last two decades of the nineteenth century and the first quarter of the twentieth, it is significant to mention that Morrison was listed as one of the workers in such camps as: Waco, Texas; Scottsville, Texas; Peniel, Texas; Bonnie, Illinois; Sychar, Ohio; Fletcher Grove, New Jersey; Hollow Rock, Ohio; Sebring, Ohio; Indian Springs, Georgia; Mt. Lake Park, Maryland; Red Rock Park, St. Paul, Minnesota; Eaton Rapids, Michigan; Winona Lake, Indiana; Wichita, Kansas; Des Plaines, Illinois, and Moores, New York. Frequently several thousand persons attended meetings during the course of the ten day campaign. Since a large number of preachers also attended, the inspiration of the camp meeting service was often carried back to their churches by them, thus greatly enlarging the influence of the evangelist. "The best results of his preaching," declared one writer in speaking of Morrison's sermons at the camp meeting held in Ocean Grove, New Jersey, "will be found in the preaching of the preachers who heard him; to them it was encouraging, comforting and stimulating, and many went home to be braver, more earnest and courageous representatives of the King of Heaven."[25]

As a preacher Morrison ranked as one of the great pulpit orators in America. Of this quality J. L. Brasher wrote:

> But great as were his many qualities, his power in the pulpit and public address was his greatest. There I watched him as he played, from instructor to advocate, and from advocate to a blast of rebuke to sin and things unholy, and then to the sweep when his eloquence took wings for great flights of fancy mixed with facts, and I, like others, said to myself: "Brother Morrison, you can get after me hammer and tongs, but I thank God for your eloquence, giving out the truth." There were tones in his

voice that I would have loved to hear for an hour, whether he was saying anything or not.[26]

A similar evaluation of Morrison's ability was made by C. F. Wimberly:

> Leaving out the personalities and the message of the man, his unusual talents of voice and other natural endowments—Henry Clay Morrison is an orator. The same messages absolutely divorced from his great Gospel theme of salvation, would meet all the specifications of the orator. Liberty, patriotism, temperance, labor leadership or whatever it might be, his voice is the voice of the true orator.
>
> We are trying to study the man as he could be, championing any other noble cause, and when we do, he must be placed among the great orators of our country; and in our humble judgment second to none—his classifications belongs, without apology or modification, with Patrick Henry, Daniel Webster, Henry W. Grady and S. S. Prentice.[27]

William Jennings Bryan is reported to have stated before a large audience, "I regard Henry Clay Morrison the greatest pulpit orator on the American Continent."[28] On one occasion Morrison introduced Bryan when he was to speak in Wilmore, Kentucky. In the introduction Morrison soared in such eulogistic flights of oratory that it drew tears to the eyes of Bryan, and when he arose to speak his words appeared commonplace and it was a number of minutes before he was able to capture the attention of his audience.

Praise for Morrison's ability as a speaker was given by those who disagreed with him as well as by his friends. Ezra L. Gillis, formerly registrar of the University of Kentucky, reported his brother as having said, "He [Morrison] is the only preacher I know that I can really enjoy listening to for an hour and a half when I do not believe anything he is saying." It was no doubt his oratorical ability which caused the *Christian Century* to number Morrison among the fifty great preachers in America. Regardless of the varied opinions as to his writings, both friend and foe agreed that Morrison was a masterful preacher.

Another avenue into which Morrison channeled his influence was the religious organizations which he sponsored. He was associated with many county, area, or state holiness associations which flourished and died, but his relationship to three is worthy of mention—the Holiness Union of the South, the Pentecostal Mission in Cuba, and the American and Evangelical Methodist Leagues of America.

None of these organizations sponsored by Morrison continued more than a few years. It appears they were not intended to do so. They were brought into being to meet a particular religious need of the time. When the scene change, outworn organizations were abandoned in order to permit a shift to more fertile methods of operation.

Morrison has been credited as being one of the most important leaders of the holiness movement. Since the National Association for the Promotion of Holiness did not project its influence into many of the Southern states, Morrison, along with other Southern holiness preachers effected the organization of the Holiness Union of the South. During the years of its operation (1904-1912), the Holiness Union gave unity to the advocates of the doctrine of entire sanctification, while at the same time encouraging loyalty to the established denominations, rather than the formation of new "holiness churches."

The Holiness Union made another contribution to the Christian emphasis through its interest in worldwide missions. For a time it assumed the support of Morrison's holiness mission enterprise in Cuba. "It was, this Holiness Union which sponsored H. C. Morrison in a world missionary tour (1909-1910), which underwrote the expenses of E. Stanley Jones during his first years as a missionary in India, and which finally aided the Cowman-Kilbourne missionary team in Japan."[29]

Immediately after the close of the Spanish-American War, Morrison became interested in improving the moral and spiritual conditions of Cuba with the result that the Pentecostal Mission in Cuba began operation in 1900. Three years later the Pentecostal Christian Church was organized, with one hundred seventy-five members. For six years this missionary enterprise was supported through gifts received largely from the constituency of *The Pentecostal Herald*. During the next two years financial backing was given by the Holiness Union; and in 1908 the Pentecostal Mission in Cuba was disbanded and the work was carried on by the mission board of the Methodist church.

Just as the rise of the holiness movement had stimulated Morrison to the organization of the holiness forces in the South, so the spread of "liberalism" led to the formation of counter movements. As early as 1916 the American Methodist League was organized for the purpose of upholding the fundamental teachings of early Methodism in opposition to the more liberal trends which were being accepted by many within the church. In 1924 the movement was reorganized under the name "Evangelical Methodist League." Its method of operation was the holding of tent meetings in which the evangelical message, as endorsed by the holiness movement, was proclaimed. The most active year for the association was in 1928, when thirty-three tents were in use and meetings were conducted over an area extending from New York to California. In sponsoring this movement he preceded its Northern counterpart, the Methodist League of Faith and Life, organized in 1925.[30] Morrison's organization continued a sporadic existence until the middle thirties when, with the waning interest in the liberalist-fundamentalist controversy, it gradually faded into non-existence.

There was probably no prominent Methodist preacher during Morrison's time who criticized the Methodist Church more severely than did he, while still retaining membership in it. At the same time there were few Methodist ministers, aside from those holding general office in the church, who had a greater influence upon Methodism than did Morrison. It has been said that no evangelist in Methodism has been given the opportunity to speak to so many preachers gathered in their Annual Conference as was he.[31] He spoke before his own Conference (the Kentucky Annual Conference) in twenty-three different sessions. In addition, he was invited to speak before the ministers of thirty-three other Annual Conferences of the Methodist Episcopal Church, South, sixteen in the Methodist Episcopal Church, two in Methodist Conferences after the union of Methodism, and to three similar ministerial gatherings of other denominations. The impact of his preaching was felt by the preachers of seventy-seven conferences.

The confidence in Morrison as held by his associates in the conference can be seen through his election as a delegate to six General Conferences of the Methodist Episcopal Church, South. In addition to his work as a delegate he was asked to speak to either the entire Conference or to some group of the Conference in all of these. In 1930, though not a delegate, Morrison was asked to preach in the Conference auditorium on two different afternoons.³² On two occasions—Los Angeles, 1904 and Baltimore, 1908—Morrison was engaged as a speaker in evangelistic services conducted during the General Conferences of the Methodist Episcopal Church. In 1936, he was invited to speak to the delegates of the General Assembly of the Church of the Nazarene, which was meeting in Kansas City.³³ Such honors came to but few men, and rarely are they repeated as frequently as in the case of H. C. Morrison.

Three other events in his life reflect the confidence which the Methodist church had in Morrison's life and ministry. First, he was elected by the College of Bishops of the Methodist Episcopal Church, South, to represent the church in the Ecumenical Conference of Methodism which met in London, England, September 6-16, 1921. To be thus selected is considered to be one of the highest honors bestowed by the church, other than the election to the bishopric. Second was his close association with the bishopric. Some of his friends approached him during the General Conference of 1918 relative to voting for him for Bishop. Instead, however, he used his influence to support the election of U. V. W. Darlington. As a result, Morrison has been given credit for being one of the factors in Darlington's election. At the General Conference of 1922, while Morrison was still basking in the glory of having been a delegate to the ecumenical conference of 1921, a number of friends again suggested electing him Bishop. One of the Bishops was said to have expressed the belief that support was strong enough to elect him, but Morrison refused to consider accepting the office even if elected.³⁴ The third event was the invitation given to Morrison by the Bishops to lead the daily testimony meeting at Trinity Methodist Church in Savannah, Georgia, during the Methodist celebration of the two hundredth anniversary of John Wesley's experience at Aldersgate. Of this great Methodist gathering, January 11-14, 1938, one preacher remarked: "Without any doubt at all, the two most talked of men in Savannah were James Cannon, Jr., and Henry C. Morrison."[35]

The influence of H. C. Morrison on the lives of young men who later rose to places of leadership in the Christian ministry is too long a story to be related here; but his relationship to the rise of Reuben "Bud" Robinson (generally known as "Uncle Bud") to a place of world renown as an evangelist is so well-known in certain church circles that to omit an account of it would be unfair.

Bud Robinson was a young, and uneducated, Texan when he was converted on August 11, 1880. He immediately felt a call to preach. Ten years later he received the baptism with the Holy Spirit as a second work of grace, but after sixteen years of trying to succeed as a preacher he was still practically unknown. It was in the summer of 1896 that Bud put his wife and baby in their farm wagon and drove to the camp meeting at Waco, Texas, in order to hear Beverly Carradine and H. C. Morrison preach. The first night of his attendance at the camp Bud was called upon to lead in prayer. That prayer drew the attention of Morrison, and he asked Bud to preach in the afternoon service on the following day. That sermon was so successful that it started Bud Robinson on the road to fame as an evangelist. At the close of his life it was said that he had traveled two million miles, preached thirty-three thousand times, had one hundred thousand seekers at his altars, had conducted revival campaigns in the churches of seventy-three denominations, had spent eighty-five thousand dollars in helping to educate young men for Christian work, and had written fourteen books of which more than a half million copies had been sold.[36] "Uncle Bud" gave much of the credit for this success to Morrison.

When I was driven to the wall in the early days, Dr. Morrison wrote me up and described me as "the Texas Wonder," and recommended me to the camp meeting committees in such camps as Terrill, Texas, Denton, Texas, Bates Camp Ground and Dublin, Texas. The surprise of my life was how a man of Dr. Morrison's ability could come down on a level with a man like I was and recommend me as his yokefellow in these battles... from the day that he championed my cause until this, I have never been able to fill the calls that I have received. Some years I have received nine hundred calls to hold meetings. Dr. Morrison deserves the credit for every one of them. He is the one man who has wisdom enough to be wise, and humility enough to be humble, and grace enough to be a saint. When he goes to heaven I know of no living man on earth who can take his place.[37]

The story of the life, theology, and influence of Henry Clay Morrison could be closed in no more fitting manner than by the presentation of tributes of his life and work by men who labored with him through the years, and by those who through their broad knowledge of the work of the entire church felt able to give an evaluation of the contributions made by him.

When Bishop H. M. DuBose wrote his *History of Methodism* he mentioned three men as being outstanding examples of Methodist evangelism in America. The three men were Samuel P. Jones, George R. Stewart, and H. C. Morrison.

In 1938, the editor of the *New York Christian Advocate* is reported to have written the following in an editorial:

> One of the great Christian personalities of American Methodism during the past fifty years has been Dr. Henry Clay Morrison of the Church, South. As an eloquent preacher of the gospel, with power to grip and hold the masses, he has few equals. Recently, at the New Jersey Annual Conference, he packed a great auditorium every day for a week. He was never sensational, but he made the gospel an amazing sensation. His sermons were unforgettable.
>
> His leadership created Asbury College, which has the right to recognition because of the mighty personalities it has sent forth into Methodism's worldwide field. Most notable among these is Dr. E. Stanley Jones, the most apostolic personality in the ranks of Christian leadership today.
>
> Then, too, Dr. Morrison has created a theological seminary, carried on evangelistic services, swayed the masses in great camp meetings clear across the nation, maintained a publishing house, and edited a church religious weekly for fifty successive years. All this he has done as an individual...The South brings no more lovely personality than his into the union of Methodism.

The Rev. Roy L. Smith, one of the leaders in Methodist Ecclesiasticism, wrote words of praise for the life and influence of Morrison.

> A tall tree has fallen in the forest, but it went down with a great shout of victory. Henry Clay

> Morrison, for fifty-nine years a member of the Kentucky Conference, died as he has lived, in the midst of a campaign for souls… we pause in the midst of a harried and tormented day to lift up our prayer of thanks for a man who lived for but one purpose—the winning of men for Jesus Christ. There were those who disagreed with him in matters of theology, but no man surpassed him in devotion to the Christian evangel. And in the midst of the sorrow occasioned by his going, tens of thousands will breathe a prayer of gratitude for the fact that his shadow fell upon their lives to heal them.[38]

Joseph H. Smith, well known Bible expositor, who was a co-worker with Morrison in many revival campaigns, gave a unique characterization of Morrison's ministry:

> Brother Morrison was an *Expositor*, rather than an Exegete. His study was not of dead languages but of the Living Word. He had no place for new versions nor trite interpretations of the Bible…With Wesley and other master ministers, he esteemed that *"anything essentially new in Religion was essentially false."*[39]

Another associate, J. L. Brasher, credited Morrison with having been one of the greatest leaders in the holiness movement. "He [Morrison] was a genius. His was a soul into which flowed many streams of information and education, and his Scotch-Irish nature held all he had taken in. Perhaps no one has done more for the spread of holiness in our lifetime than he has."[40]

George W. Ridout, formerly a professor in Asbury College, and for years a contributing editor of *The Herald*, spoke of Morrison's qualities as a crusading warrior.

> To him was given by Nature and Nature's God a heart to move the multitude, a mind to think God's thoughts, a voice to rouse his century, his church and his country.
>
> Dr. Morrison was endowed with the prophet's vision and fire; the warrior's courage and daring, and the passion of the soul winner. His time and age felt the impact of his great soul...
>
> He was one of God's servants who faced danger for the Truth's sake, feared not the cost of sacrifice and toil. He early forsook softness and ease for the battle front....
>
> To Dr. Morrison religion was a passion and the ministry a crusade, not a profession... [He] became to Methodism, especially, the peculiar gift of God at a time when doubt and discount were playing havoc with the great doctrines of perfect love. As a good soldier he unsheathed the sword in defense of sound doctrine, he fought a good fight, broke down walls of opposition, and became the leader of hosts of men whose hearts God had touched. Southern Methodism shall never forget what Henry Clay Morrison did to set the gospel of full salvation to a new tune and give it a happier place among the churches.[41]

As his part of the funeral service for Morrison, Dr. Paul S. Rees, a pastor-evangelist well known among the holiness churches in America, spoke of Morrison as a preacher-prophet, a preacher-priest, and a preacher-king.

> Dr. Morrison was a *preacher-prophet*. He interpreted God to men in the very best traditions of the prophetic office. His sermons were not polished. homilies, reminding one of exquisitely chased silver. They were rather volcanic deliverances. Someone asked Father Taylor for a definition of preaching. He replied: "Preaching is taking something hot out of the heart of God and shoving it into mine." That was Dr. Morrison in action.

> ....

> Dr. Morrison was a *preacher-priest*. He not only interpreted God to men, he brought men near to God. He led them in worship with an impressiveness and contagiousness that few can command. He was the very embodiment of reverence... His prayers were golden elevators by which all those who were within their hearing were raised up, up! UP!! to the very bleeding heart of Christ...

> Dr. Morrison was a *preacher-king*. His very appearance said so. The pulpit was his throne. Both nature and personal taste combined to make him look the regal part. Yet there was nothing like artificial posing about him. Dr. Morrison was not two men—one in the pulpit and another out of it. He was one man, and that one was always preaching.[42]

Bishop Arthur J. Moore, who at one time was reported to have said that his ministry was typed more by H. C. Morrison than by any other man, rated Morrison as the greatest champion of entire sanctification within Methodism.

Throughout his lifetime he was the exponent and champion of the Wesleyan doctrine of entire sanctification as a second work of grace. He not only proclaimed but exhibited in his life this doctrine of perfect love. To him, more than to any other one man, we are indebted for keeping this original standard of Methodism alive in the modern church...[43]

During the funeral service for H. C. Morrison, tribute was paid to him as a churchman by Bishop U. V. W. Darlington. While speaking of Morrison and his relationship to the Methodist church he said, "I doubt if the death of any one man in Methodism brings so much sorrow as this. I doubt if there is a man in the world who has meant more to so many people."[44]

A quotation from an address made at Asbury College on May 8, 1942, by E. Stanley Jones, in which he not only gives an evaluation of the life and work of Henry Clay Morrison, but also offers a challenge to Christian workers whose lives shall reach into the tomorrows, serves as the closing paragraph of this study.

> I need not tell you what you have told yourselves a hundred times since the passing of Dr. Morrison, that one of the great men of the religious life of America has passed from us, the last of the old Southern orators. There will never be another Southern orator like him, I suppose. It was in his blood, in his frame, in his make-up. He was set on fire by the experience of the Spirit of God and therefore for eighty-five

years he wrote and taught. When he fell at last there was a great vacancy upon the horizon, as if a great oak tree had gone and left a vacancy. Yet, as I stood beside his grave this afternoon.... [I] prayed that the mantle of his life might fall upon some of the rest of us. We will not have his gift of oratory, and perhaps the tastes of the age change, but that single minded fervor, that one pointedness of mind, that one holding to a goal through thick and thin, where a man could say, "this one thing I do," that passion to lead men to Christ, can fall upon us.[45]

Notes

[1] J. L. Brasher, *Glimpses* (Cincinnati, 1954). Hereafter referred to as *Glimpses*.

[2] "Asbury Alumni Questionnaire."

[3] *The Pentecostal Herald.*

[4] *Ibid.*

[5] J. J. Dickey, "Diary."

[6] *The Pentecostal Herald.*

[7] *Ibid.*

[8] *Catalogue of Asbury College.*

[9] *The Cadle Call.*

[10] *The Pentecostal Herald.*

[11] J. J. Dickey, "Diary."

[12] *The Cadle Call.*

[13] *Ibid.*

[14] Letter to the author from S. E. McCreless, April 22, 1954.

[15] *The Pentecostal Herald.*

[16] *The Cadle Call.*

[17] Federal Security Agency Office of Education, Circular No. 248, Nov. 14, 1948.

[18] Persons quoted were: Willis Shehan Parker, O. C. Mingledorff, Gene E. Phillips, Paul G. Keller, and Don A. Morris.

[19] *Ibid.*

[20] *Ibid.*

[21] *Ibid.*

[22] *Ibid.*

[23] *Glimpses.*

[24] *The Pentecostal Herald.*

[25] *Ibid.*

[26] *Glimpses.*

[27] *A Biographical Sketch of Henry Clay Morrison.*

[28] "Conference Minutes."

[29] Delbert R. Rose, "The Theology of Joseph H. Smith" (Unpublished Ph. D. dissertation, University of Iowa, 1952).

[30] *Methodism in American History.*

[31] *The Pentecostal Herald.*

[32] H. C. Morrison, "Diary," 1893, 1895-1910; 1913-41.

[33] *Ibid.*

[34] *Ibid.*

[35] *The Pentecostal Herald.*

[36] *Ibid.*

[37] *Ibid.*

[38] *The Christian Advocate.*

[39] *The Pentecostal Herald.*

[40] *Glimpses.*

[41] *The Pentecostal Herald.*

[42] "Stenographic Records."

[43] *The Pentecostal Herald.*

[44] "Stenographic Records."

[45] *Ibid.*

www.ingramcontent.com/pod-product-compliance
Lightning Source LLC
Chambersburg PA
CBHW061428040426
42450CB00007B/942